MACARTHUR
BIBLE STUDIES

1 CORINTHIANS

Godly Solutions for Church Problems

JOHN
MacARTHUR

1 CORINTHIANS
MACARTHUR BIBLE STUDIES

The quotes from John MacArthur in the "Summing Up" sections are from *MacArthur New Testament Commentary: 1 Corinthians* (Moody Press: Chicago, IL, 1984). Used by permission. All rights reserved.

Scripture passages taken from:
The Holy Bible, *New King James Version*
Copyright © 1979, 1980, 1982 by Thomas Nelson. All rights reserved.

Cover Art by The Puckett Group.
Interior design and composition by Design Corps, Batavia, IL.

Produced with the assistance of the Livingstone Corporation. Project staff include Dave Veerman, Christopher D. Hudson, and Amber Rae.

Project editor: Len Woods

ISBN 0-8499-5551-3

02 03 04 PHX 5 4

1 Corinthians

Table of Contents

THE FIRST EPISTLE OF PAUL TO THE CORINTHIANS

Introduction

The letter is named for the city of Corinth, where the church to whom it was written was located. With the exception of personal epistles addressed to Timothy, Titus, and Philemon, all Paul's letters bear the name of the city where the church addressed existed.

Author and Date

As indicated in the first verse, the epistle was written by the Apostle Paul, whose authorship cannot be seriously questioned. Pauline authorship has been universally accepted by the church since the first century, when 1 Corinthians was penned. Internally, the apostle claimed to have written the epistle (1:1, 13; 3:4–6; 4:15; 16:21). Externally, this correspondence has been acknowledged as genuine since A.D. 95 by Clement of Rome, who was writing to the Corinthian church. Other early Christian leaders who authenticated Paul as author include Ignatius (about A.D. 110), Polycarp (about A.D. 135), and Tertullian (about A.D. 200).

This epistle was most likely written in the first half of A.D. 55 from Ephesus (16:8–9, 19) while Paul was on his third missionary journey. The apostle intended to remain at Ephesus to complete his three-year stay (Acts 20:31) until Pentecost (May/June) A.D. 55 (16:8). Then he hoped to winter (A.D. 55–56) at Corinth (16:6; Acts 20:2). His departure for Corinth was anticipated even as he wrote (4:19; 11:34; 16:8).

Background and Setting

The city of Corinth was located in southern Greece, in what was the Roman province of Achaia, about forty-five miles west of Athens. This lower part, the Peloponnesus, is connected to the rest of Greece by a four-mile-wide isthmus, which is bounded on the east by the Saronic Gulf and on the west by the Gulf of Corinth. Corinth is near the middle of the isthmus and is prominently situated on a high plateau. For many centuries, all north-south land traffic in that area had to pass through or near this ancient city. Since travel by sea around the Peloponnesus involved a 250-mile voyage that was dangerous and time consuming, most captains carried their ships on skids or rollers across the isthmus directly past Corinth. Corinth understandably prospered as a major trade city, not only for most of Greece but for much of the Mediterranean area, including North Africa, Italy, and Asia Minor. A canal across the isthmus was begun by the emperor Nero during the first century A.D. but was not completed until near the end of the nineteenth century.

The Isthmian games, one of the two most famous athletic events of that day (the other being the Olympic games), were hosted by Corinth, causing more people-traffic. Even by the pagan standards of its own culture, Corinth became so morally corrupt that its very name became synonymous with debauchery and moral depravity. To "corinthianize" came to represent gross immorality and drunken debauchery. In 6:9–10, Paul lists some of the specific sins for which the city was noted and which formerly had characterized many believers in the church there. Tragically, some of the worst sins were still found among church members. One of those sins, incest, was condemned even by most pagan Gentiles (5:1).

Like most ancient Greek cities, Corinth had an acropolis (literally "a high city"), which rose two thousand feet and was used both for defense and for worship. The most prominent edifice on the acropolis was a temple to Aphrodite, the Greek goddess of love. About a thousand priestesses, who were "religious" prostitutes, lived and worked there and came down into the city in the evening to offer their services to male citizens and foreign visitors.

The church in Corinth was founded by Paul on his second missionary journey (Acts 18:1ff.). As usual, his ministry began in the synagogue, where he was assisted by two Jewish believers, Priscilla and Aquila, with whom he lived for a while and who were fellow tradesmen. Soon after, Silas and Timothy joined them, and Paul began preaching even more intensely in the synagogue. When most of the Jews resisted the gospel, he left the synagogue, but not before Crispus, the leader of the synagogue, his family, and many other Corinthians were converted (Acts 18:5–8).

After ministering in Corinth for over a year and a half (Acts 18:11), Paul was brought before a Roman tribunal by some of the Jewish leaders. Because the charges were strictly religious and not civil, the proconsul, Gallio, dismissed the case. Shortly thereafter, Paul took Priscilla and Aquila with him to Ephesus. From there he returned to Israel (vv. 18–22).

Unable to fully break with the culture from which it came, the church at Corinth was exceptionally factional, showing its carnality and immaturity. After the gifted Apollos had ministered in the church for some time, a group of his admirers established a clique and had little to do with the rest of the church. Another group developed that was loyal to Paul, another claimed special allegiance to Peter (Cephas), and still another to Christ alone (see 1:10–13; 3:1–9).

The most serious problem of the Corinthian church was worldliness, an unwillingness to divorce the culture around them. Most of the believers could not consistently separate themselves from their old, selfish, immoral, and pagan ways. It became necessary for Paul to write to correct this, as well as to command the faithful Christians not only to break fellowship with the disobedient and unrepentant members, but to put those members out of the church (5:9–13).

Before he wrote this inspired letter, Paul had written the church other correspondence (see 5:9), which was also corrective in nature. Because a copy of that letter has never been discovered, it has been referred to as "the lost epistle." There was another non-canonical letter after 1 Corinthians, usually called "the severe letter" (2 Cor. 2:4).

Historical and Theological Themes

Although the major thrust of this epistle is corrective of behavior rather than of doctrine, Paul explains many doctrines that directly relate to the matters of sin and righteousness. In one way or another, wrong living always stems from wrong belief. Sexual sins, for example, including divorce, are inevitably related to lack of belief or trust in God's plan for marriage and the family (7:1–40). Proper worship is determined by such things as recognition of God's holy character (3:17), the spiritual identity of the church (12:12–27), and pure partaking of the Lord's Supper (11:17–34). It is not possible for the church to be edified faithfully and effectively unless believers understand and exercise their spiritual gifts (12:1–14:40). The importance of the doctrine of the resurrection, of course, cannot be overestimated, because if there is no resurrection of the dead, then Christ is not risen. And if Christ is not risen, then preaching is empty and so is faith (15:13–14).

In addition to those themes, Paul deals briefly with God's judgment of believers, the right understanding of which will produce right motives for godly living (see 3:13–15). The right understanding of idols and of false gods, in general, was to help the immature Corinthians think maturely about such things as eating meat that had been sacrificed to idols (8:1–11:1). The right understanding and expression of genuine, godly love was mandatory to right use of the gifts and even to right knowledge about all the things of God (13:1–13).

So Paul deals with the cross, divine wisdom and human wisdom, the work of the Spirit in illumination, carnality, eternal rewards, the transformation of salvation, sanctification, the nature of Christ, union with Him, the divine role for women, marriage and divorce, Spirit baptism, indwelling and gifting, the unity of the church in one body, the theology of love, and the doctrine of resurrection. All these establish foundational truth for godly behavior.

Interpretive Challenges

By far the most controversial issue for interpretation is that of the sign gifts discussed in chapters 12–14, particularly the gifts of miracles and tongues-speaking. Many believe that all the gifts are permanent, so that the gift of speaking in tongues will cease (13:8) only at the time the gifts of prophecy and of knowledge cease, namely, when that which is perfect has come (v. 10). Those who maintain that tongues and miracles are still valid spiritual gifts in the church today believe they should be exercised with the same power they were in New Testament times by the apostles. Others believe the miraculous sign gifts have ceased. This controversy will be touched on in the appropriate notes on chapters 12–14.

The issue of divorce is a troubling one for many. Chapter 7 addresses the subject but calls for careful interpretation to yield consistent biblical doctrine on the matter.

Advocates of universalism, the idea that all men will eventually be saved, use 15:22 in support of that view, claiming that, just as every human being died spiritually because of Adam's sin, they will all be saved through Christ's righteousness. The note on that verse will confront the challenge of such universalists.

From that same chapter, the obscure phrase "baptized for the dead" (v. 29) has been used to defend the notion that a dead person can be saved by being baptized vicariously through a living Christian. There have been over forty suggested explanations for this baptism. As the notes will point out, regardless of how that particular verse is interpreted, the falsehood of dead people having the opportunity to be saved is proven by many other texts that are indisputably clear.

A much less serious issue concerns the meaning of 6:4, which pertains to Christians taking other Christians to court before unbelievers. The resolution of that problem lies primarily in being obedient to another verse that is itself unambiguous.

OUTLINE

I. Introduction: The Calling and Benefits of Sainthood (1:1–9)
II. Disunity in the Church (1:10–4:21)
    A. The Need for Unity (1:10–3:23)
    B. The Need for Servanthood (4:1–21)
III. Immorality in the Church (5:1–6:20)
IV. Marriage in the Church (7:1–40)
V. Liberty in the Church (8:1–11:1)
VI. Worship in the Church (11:2–14:40)
    A. Roles of Men and Women in the Church (11:2–16)
    B. The Lord's Supper (11:17–34)
    C. Spiritual Gifts (12:1–4:40)
VII. The Hope of the Church: Resurrection (15:1–58)
VIII. A Charge to the Church (16:1–24)
    A. Stewardship (16:1–4)
    B. Personal Plans and Greetings (16:5–24)

Called To Be Saints

1 Corinthians 1:1–9

Opening Thought

1) Who or what are you most thankful for and why?

God for sending His son to save us. My family; my parents for a great role model and support, my wife and daughter for getting me focused and making me laugh.

2) Other than "Christian," what are some words often used to describe those who believe in Christ?

Believers, brothers & sisters, children of God, Sons & daughters, saints

3) Is it hard for you to think of yourself as a "saint"? Why or why not?

Yes, simply for the fact of the Catholic use of the term, I don't feel I'm good enough

4) When you are required to say hard things to someone, how do you typically go about it?

Try to be gentle and usually find out the background in their situation and life so as to be understanding.

Background of the Passage

It is important to establish one's right to speak authoritatively on a subject. A person, for instance, who has no medical degree or training or experience would never get a hearing at a conference on medicine. A person's credentials give some indication as to whether or not what he has to say should be taken seriously. Paul did not mention his apostleship in order to gain honor as an individual but to gain respect as a teacher of God's Word. He was not an apostle by his own appointment, or even by the church's appointment, but by God's appointment—by the will of God. At the outset (v. 1) he wanted to establish that what he had to say was said with God's own authority. Since his message was so corrective, this was of great necessity.

Before Paul took the Corinthians to task for their failures as Christians, he carefully and lovingly reminded them that they were Christians. They belonged to God and to each other in a far-reaching fellowship. In verses 2–9 he summarizes their position and their blessings as believers in Jesus Christ, as children of God, as saints. The benefits of being a Christian have three dimensions. Some are past, given the moment we accept Christ as Savior and Lord. Others are present, worked out as we live our lives in Him. Still others are future, to be experienced only when we go to be with Him in heaven. In the past there is grace, in the present there are gifts, and for the future there are guarantees. Our past is already taken care of, our present is provided for, and our future is assured. In so many words, Paul is saying: "Look at what you are! Look at what you have!" Only then does he say, "Now I exhort you, brethren" (1:10).

Bible Passage

Read 1 Corinthians 1:1–9, noting the key words and definitions to the right of the passage.

1 Corinthians 1:1–9

¹ *Paul, called to be an apostle of Jesus Christ through the will of God, and Sosthenes our brother,*

² *To the church of God which is at Corinth, to those who are sanctified in Christ Jesus, called to be saints, with all who in every place call on the name of Jesus Christ our Lord, both theirs and ours:*

apostle (v. 1)—Literally, "a sent one." Paul establishes his authority as an emissary of the Lord Jesus by God's appointment (9:1; 15:8), made especially necessary because so much of the message of this epistle is corrective (2:1–7). Since he was delegated by God to speak and write, resisting him was resisting God.

Sosthenes (v. 1)—probably Paul's secretary, a former leader of the

³ *Grace to you and peace from God our Father and the Lord Jesus Christ.*

⁴ *I thank my God always concerning you for the grace of God which was given to you by Christ Jesus,*

⁵ *that you were enriched in everything by Him in all utterance and all knowledge,*

⁶ *even as the testimony of Christ was confirmed in you,*

⁷ *so that you come short in no gift, eagerly waiting for the revelation of our Lord Jesus Christ,*

⁸ *who will also confirm you to the end, that you may be blameless in the day of our Lord Jesus Christ.*

⁹ *God is faithful, by whom you were called into the fellowship of His Son, Jesus Christ our Lord.*

Corinthian synagogue who had become a brother in Christ; on one occasion, he was beaten for bringing Paul before the civil court at Corinth (Acts 18:12–17)

saints (v. 2)—not referring to a specially pious or revered person canonized by an ecclesiastical body, but a reference to everyone who by salvation has been sanctified, that is, set apart from sin in Christ Jesus

Grace to you and peace (v. 3) —Paul used this greeting in all his letters. The basic meaning of "grace" is favor; "peace" is inner wholeness and right relations with God and others as a result of God's saving grace.

grace of God . . . given (v. 4)— This looks at the past, that is, their salvation, when God justified them by undeserved and unrepayable love and mercy, forgiving their sin through the work of His Son.

enriched in everything by Him (v. 5)—In the present, the believer has everything the Lord has to give and therefore everything he needs. The two particular blessings spoken of here are related to presenting the truth of God's Word.

utterance (v. 5)—In regard to speaking for God, believers are able to speak when God wants them to because of His enablement. Prayer reaches out for that ability, and diligence in the study of God's Word aids it.

all knowledge (v. 5)—God provides believers with all the knowledge they need in order to speak effectively for Him (see 2:9).

testimony of Christ . . . confirmed in you (v. 6)—This is a reference to the moment of salvation when the gospel was heard and believed and settled in the heart. At that moment, the enabling of verse 4 took place, because the individual became a recipient of the grace of God.

come short in no gift (v. 7)— "Gift" in Greek is specifically "a gift of grace." While the blessings of speech and knowledge were primarily for evangelizing the lost, the spiritual gifts (chaps. 12–14) edify the church. Because these gifts are given to each believer (12:11–12) without regard for maturity or spirituality, the Corinthians, though sinful, had them in full.

the revelation (v. 7)—Paul looks to the blessing of future grace. At the Lord's second coming, His full glory, honor, and majesty will be revealed in blazing splendor (Rev. 4:11; 5:12), at which time all true believers will be fixed solidly forever as holy and without sin, in full resurrected glory and purity, to live in heaven with God forever.

the day of our Lord Jesus Christ (v. 8)—See 5:5. This refers to the coming of the Lord for His church, the rapture. This is to be distinguished from the Day of the Lord (1 Thess. 5:2, 4; 2 Thess. 2:2), a term referring to judgment on the ungodly.

God is faithful (v. 9)—Because of God's sovereign and unchangeable promise, believers are assured of this grace—past, present, and future—and will remain saved, assured of future glory at Christ's appearing (Eph. 5:26–27).

by whom you were called (v. 9)—This call, as always in the epistles of the New Testament, refers to an effectual call that saves (see note on Rom. 8:30). God who calls to salvation and heaven will be faithful to give the grace needed to fulfill that call.

Understanding the Text

5) What did Paul mean when he called the Corinthian believers saints?

Everyone who was saved by Jesus

(verses to consider: Heb. 10:10, 14; 2 Pet. 1:3; Jude 1)

6) Paul thanked God for what specific things in the lives of the Corinthians?

grace

7) In what ways had the Corinthians been enriched by Christ?

through all utterance and knowledge

(verses to consider: 1 Cor.3:21; Eph. 1:3; Col. 2:10; 2 Pet. 1:3)

8) How did Paul say the Corinthians would be able to live as God desired?

coming short in no gift

Cross Reference

Read Ephesians 1:1–14.

¹ *Paul, an apostle of Jesus Christ by the will of God,*
    To the saints who are in Ephesus, and faithful in Christ Jesus:

2 *Grace to you and peace from God our Father and the Lord Jesus Christ.*

3 *Blessed be the God and Father of our Lord Jesus Christ, who has blessed us with every spiritual blessing in the heavenly places in Christ,*

4 *just as He chose us in Him before the foundation of the world, that we should be holy and without blame before Him in love,*

5 *having predestined us to adoption as sons by Jesus Christ to Himself, according to the good pleasure of His will,*

6 *to the praise of the glory of His grace, by which He has made us accepted in the Beloved.*

7 *In Him we have redemption through His blood, the forgiveness of sins, according to the riches of His grace*

8 *which He made to abound toward us in all wisdom and prudence,*

9 *having made known to us the mystery of His will, according to His good pleasure which He purposed in Himself,*

10 *that in the dispensation of the fullness of the times He might gather together in one all things in Christ, both which are in heaven and which are on earth—in Him.*

11 *In Him also we have obtained an inheritance, being predestined according to the purpose of Him who works all things according to the counsel of His will,*

12 *that we who first trusted in Christ should be to the praise of His glory.*

13 *In Him you also trusted, after you heard the word of truth, the gospel of your salvation; in whom also, having believed, you were sealed with the Holy Spirit of promise,*

14 *who is the guarantee of our inheritance until the redemption of the purchased possession, to the praise of His glory.*

Exploring the Meaning

9) What does this passage reveal about the benefits of grace?

We are accepted, forgiven.

10) Read John 14:1–3. How did the promise of Christ's return affect Paul's teaching, his ministry philosophy, and his behavior?

He let his worldly troubles go and focused on God preparing

(verses to consider: 1 Thess. 4:13–18; Rev. 3:10)   _a room for him in Heaven_

11) Read 1 John 1:3–7. What does this say about the life to which God has called believers?

That if we want to be true children of God we must give up sin and follow Christ.

(verses to look at: Rom. 8:30; 1 Thess. 5:23)

Summing Up . . .

"As Christians, one of the strongest rebukes we can have when we sin is to be reminded of who our Father is. And reminding ourselves of whose we are should be one of our strongest deterrents to sin. Remembering our position can compel us to improve our practice."—*John MacArthur*

Reflecting on the Text

12) What "past" benefits of grace are you most thankful for?

_____

13) What "present" benefits of grace do you most appreciate?

_____

14) What "future" benefits of grace do you most anticipate?

_____

15) What specific things can you stop doing or start doing today to better demonstrate your sainthood?

_____

Recording Your Thoughts

_____

_____

For further study, see the following passages:

Matthew 11:15	John 14:27	Acts 4:29, 31
Acts 9:3–6, 17	Acts 22:11–15	Romans 1:1
2 Corinthians 1:14	2 Corinthians 4:6	2 Corinthians 11:2
Ephesians 4:11	Ephesians 5:25–27	Ephesians 6:19
Philippians 4:7	Col. 1:9–10	2 Timothy 3:15
1 Peter 3:15	Revelation 17:14	

The Need for Unity

Opening Thought

1) Give an example or personal illustration of each of the following:

• the most ridiculous argument or silliest squabble you've ever been a part of

• the most serious or damaging church conflict you've ever seen

• a situation in which you saw opposing parties settle their differences and find harmony

• a time when you saw Christians break fellowship over a doctrinal issue

2) What are some aspects of the Christian gospel that seemed foolish to you before you turned in faith to Christ? that seem foolish to the watching world?

_____

_____

3) How would you define the phrase "the wisdom of God"?

_____

_____

4) What's the greatest prize or honor you've ever won or received?

_____

_____

Background of the Passage

Most of us who have attended church for a number of years have been in or know of a congregation where there was a split or at least serious quarreling. The problem has existed in the church from New Testament times. The Corinthian believers fell short of the Lord's standards in many ways, and the first thing for which Paul called them to task was quarreling.

Quarreling is a reality in the church because selfishness and other sins are realities in the church. Because of quarreling the Father is dishonored, the Son is disgraced, His people are demoralized and discredited, and the world is turned off and confirmed in unbelief.

In His high priestly prayer the Lord prayed repeatedly that His church would be one (John 17:11, 21–23). Immediately after Pentecost the newly empowered believers were in perfect harmony with each other—sharing, rejoicing, worshiping, and witnessing together. Their unity bore great fruit in their ministry to each other, in their witness to the world, and in their pleasing and glorifying God.

The first need of the Corinthian church was for that sort of harmony. And so Paul made a plea for doctrinal agreement, for repenting of their tendency to form factions around high-profile personalities, and for remembering the great priority of the church: preaching the gospel. Paul argued that supernatural unity can occur only when God's wisdom is valued over earthly wisdom (1:18–2:16), and when believers walk in the power of God's spirit rather than giving in to the sinful desires of human flesh (3:1–23).

Bible Passage

Read 1 Corinthians 1:10–3:23, noting the key words and definitions to the right of the passage.

1 Corinthians 1:10–3:23

¹⁰ *Now I plead with you, brethren, by the name of our Lord Jesus Christ, that you all speak the same thing, and that there be no divisions among you, but that you be perfectly joined together in the same mind and in the same judgment.*
¹¹ *For it has been declared to me concerning you,*

speak the same thing (v. 10) — Paul is emphasizing the unity of doctrine in the local assembly of believers, not the spiritual unity of His universal church. Doctrinal unity, clearly and completely based on Scripture, must be the foundation of all church life. Both weak commitment to doctrine and commitment to disunity of doctrine will severely weaken a church and destroy true unity. In its place, there can be only

14

my brethren, by those of Chloe's household, that there are contentions among you.

12 Now I say this, that each of you says, "I am of Paul," or "I am of Apollos," or "I am of Cephas," or "I am of Christ."

13 Is Christ divided? Was Paul crucified for you? Or were you baptized in the name of Paul?

14 I thank God that I baptized none of you except Crispus and Gaius,

15 lest anyone should say that I had baptized in my own name.

16 Yes, I also baptized the household of Stephanas. Besides, I do not know whether I baptized any other.

17 For Christ did not send me to baptize, but to preach the gospel, not with wisdom of words, lest the cross of Christ should be made of no effect.

18 For the message of the cross is foolishness to those who are perishing, but to us who are being saved it is the power of God.

19 For it is written:
"I will destroy the wisdom of the wise,
And bring to nothing the understanding of the prudent."

20 Where is the wise? Where is the scribe? Where is the disputer of this age? Has not God made foolish the wisdom of this world?

21 For since, in the wisdom of God, the world through wisdom did not know God, it pleased God through the foolishness of the message preached to save those who believe.

22 For Jews request a sign, and Greeks seek after wisdom;

23 but we preach Christ crucified, to the Jews a stumbling block and to the Greeks foolishness,

24 but to those who are called, both Jews and Greeks, Christ the power of God and the wisdom of God.

25 Because the foolishness of God is wiser than men, and the weakness of God is stronger than men.

shallow sentimentalism or superficial harmony.

joined together (v. 10)—The basic idea is that of putting back together something that was broken or separated so it is no longer divided. The term is used in both the New Testament and in classical Greek to speak of mending such things as nets, broken bones or utensils, torn garments, and dislocated joints.

same mind . . . same judgment (v. 10)—The demand is for unity internally in their individual minds and externally in decisions made among themselves—unified in truth by beliefs, convictions, standards, and in behavior by applied principles of living. The only source of such unity is God's Word, which establishes the standard of truth on which true unity rests.

there are contentions among you (vv. 11–13)—See 3:4–8.

Chloe's household (v. 11)—Probably a prominent woman in the Corinthian church who had written or come to visit Paul in Ephesus to tell him of the factions in the church.

Apollos (v. 12)—See notes on 16:12 and Acts 18:24–28.

Cephas (v. 12)—the Apostle Peter

Is Christ divided? (v. 13)—No human leader, not even an apostle, should be given the loyalty that belongs only to the Lord. Such elevation of leaders leads only to contention, disputes, and a divided church. Christ is not divided and neither is His body, the church. Paul depreciates his worth in comparison to the Lord Jesus. For more on unity, see 12:12–13.

Crispus (v. 14)—The leader of the synagogue in Corinth, who was converted under Paul's preaching (Acts 18:8). His conversion led to that of many others.

Gaius (v. 14)—Since Romans was written from Corinth, this man was probably the host referred to in Romans 16:23.

26 *For you see your calling, brethren, that not many wise according to the flesh, not many mighty, not many noble, are called.*

27 *But God has chosen the foolish things of the world to put to shame the wise, and God has chosen the weak things of the world to put to shame the things which are mighty;*

28 *and the base things of the world and the things which are despised God has chosen, and the things which are not, to bring to nothing the things that are,*

29 *that no flesh should glory in His presence.*

30 *But of Him you are in Christ Jesus, who became for us wisdom from God—and righteousness and sanctification and redemption—*

31 *that, as it is written, "He who glories, let him glory in the LORD."*

2:1 *And I, brethren, when I came to you, did not come with excellence of speech or of wisdom declaring to you the testimony of God.*

2 *For I determined not to know anything among you except Jesus Christ and Him crucified.*

3 *I was with you in weakness, in fear, and in much trembling.*

4 *And my speech and my preaching were not with persuasive words of human wisdom, but in demonstration of the Spirit and of power,*

5 *that your faith should not be in the wisdom of men but in the power of God.*

6 *However, we speak wisdom among those who are mature, yet not the wisdom of this age, nor of the rulers of this age, who are coming to nothing.*

7 *But we speak the wisdom of God in a mystery, the hidden wisdom which God ordained before the ages for our glory,*

8 *which none of the rulers of this age knew; for had they known, they would not have crucified the Lord of glory.*

Stephanas (v. 16)—Nothing is known of this family.

Christ did not send me to baptize (v. 17)—This verse does not mean that people should not be baptized (see Acts 2:38), but that God did not send Paul to start a private cult of people personally baptized by him. He was called to preach the gospel and bring people to oneness in Christ, not baptize a faction around himself.

message of the cross (v. 18)—God's total revelation, that is, the gospel in all its fullness, which centers in the incarnation and crucifixion of Christ (2:2); the entire divine plan and provision for the redemption of sinners, which is the theme of all Scripture, is in view

foolishness (v. 18)—translates the word from which "moron" is derived

perishing . . . being saved (v. 18)—Every person is in either the process of salvation (which is not completed until the redemption of the body; see Rom. 8:23) or the process of destruction. One's response to the cross of Christ determines which. To the Christ-rejectors who are in the process of being destroyed, the gospel is non-sense. To those who are believers it is powerful wisdom.

it is written (v. 19)—Quoted from Isaiah 29:14 (see note there) to emphasize that man's wisdom will be destroyed. Isaiah's prophecy will have its ultimate fulfillment in the last days when Christ sets up His kingdom and all of human wisdom comes to an end.

Where is the wise? (v. 20)—Paul paraphrased Isaiah 19:12, where the prophet was referring to the wise men of Egypt who promised, but never produced, wisdom. Human wisdom always proves to be unreliable and impermanent (see v. 17).

scribe (v. 20)—Probably Paul has in mind the Assyrians, who sent scribes along with their soldiers to

⁹ But as it is written:
"Eye has not seen, nor ear heard,
Nor have entered into the heart of man
The things which God has prepared for those who
love Him."

¹⁰ But God has revealed them to us through His Spirit. For the Spirit searches all things, yes, the deep things of God.

¹¹ For what man knows the things of a man except the spirit of the man which is in him? Even so no one knows the things of God except the Spirit of God.

¹² Now we have received, not the spirit of the world, but the Spirit who is from God, that we might know the things that have been freely given to us by God.

¹³ These things we also speak, not in words which man's wisdom teaches but which the Holy Spirit teaches, comparing spiritual things with spiritual.

¹⁴ But the natural man does not receive the things of the Spirit of God, for they are foolishness to him; nor can he know them, because they are spiritually discerned.

¹⁵ But he who is spiritual judges all things, yet he himself is rightly judged by no one.

¹⁶ For "who has known the mind of the LORD that he may instruct Him?" But we have the mind of Christ.

³:¹ And I, brethren, could not speak to you as to spiritual people but as to carnal, as to babes in Christ.

² I fed you with milk and not with solid food; for until now you were not able to receive it, and even now you are still not able;

³ for you are still carnal. For where there are envy, strife, and divisions among you, are you not carnal and behaving like mere men?

⁴ For when one says, "I am of Paul," and another, "I am of Apollos," are you not carnal?

record the booty taken in battle. God saw to it they had nothing to record.

disputer (v. 20)—This was a Greek word with no Old Testament counterpart, identifying those who were adept at arguing philosophy.

in the wisdom of God (v. 21)—God wisely established that men could not come to know Him by human wisdom. That would exalt man, so God designed to save helpless sinners through the preaching of a message that was so simple the "worldly wise" deemed it nonsense.

who believe (v. 21)—From the human side, salvation requires and comes only through faith.

a sign (v. 22)—Unbelieving Jews still wanted supernatural signs, yet they refused to accept the most glorious of all the supernatural signworks of God, the provision of salvation through a virgin-born, crucified, and risen Messiah. In fact, the sign was a stumbling block to them (see Rom. 9:31–33).

wisdom (v. 22)—Gentiles wanted proof by means of human reason, through ideas they could set forth, discuss, and debate. Like the Athenian philosophers, they were not sincere, with no interest in divine truth, but merely wanting to argue intellectual novelty.

Christ crucified (v. 23)—The only true sign and the only true wisdom. This alone was the message Paul would preach (2:2) because it alone had the power to save all who believed.

called (vv. 24–25)—See note on v. 9. To all the "called," the message of the cross, which seems so pointless and irrelevant to man's proud, natural mind, actually exhibits God's greatest power and greatest wisdom.

God has chosen the foolish things (v. 27)—God disdained human wisdom, not only by disallowing it as a means to knowing Him, but also by choosing to save the lowly. He does not call to salva-

⁵ Who then is Paul, and who is Apollos, but ministers through whom you believed, as the Lord gave to each one?

⁶ I planted, Apollos watered, but God gave the increase.

⁷ So then neither he who plants is anything, nor he who waters, but God who gives the increase.

⁸ Now he who plants and he who waters are one, and each one will receive his own reward according to his own labor.

⁹ For we are God's fellow workers; you are God's field, you are God's building.

¹⁰ According to the grace of God which was given to me, as a wise master builder I have laid the foundation, and another builds on it. But let each one take heed how he builds on it.

¹¹ For no other foundation can anyone lay than that which is laid, which is Jesus Christ.

¹² Now if anyone builds on this foundation with gold, silver, precious stones, wood, hay, straw,

¹³ each one's work will become clear; for the Day will declare it, because it will be revealed by fire; and the fire will test each one's work, of what sort it is.

¹⁴ If anyone's work which he has built on it endures, he will receive a reward.

¹⁵ If anyone's work is burned, he will suffer loss; but he himself will be saved, yet so as through fire.

¹⁶ Do you not know that you are the temple of God and that the Spirit of God dwells in you?

¹⁷ If anyone defiles the temple of God, God will destroy him. For the temple of God is holy, which temple you are.

¹⁸ Let no one deceive himself. If anyone among you seems to be wise in this age, let him become a fool that he may become wise.

¹⁹ For the wisdom of this world is foolishness with God. For it is written, "He catches the wise in their own craftiness";

tion many whom the world would call wise, mighty, and noble (see Matt. 18:3–4). God's wisdom is revealed to the foolish, weak, and common, that is, those considered nothing by the elite, who trust in Jesus Christ as Savior and Lord. God clearly received all the credit and the glory for causing such lowly ones to know Him and the eternal truths of His heavenly kingdom. No saved sinner can boast that he has achieved salvation by his intellect (v. 29).

He who glories (v. 31)—quoted from Jeremiah 9:24

excellence of speech or of wisdom (v. 1)—See 1:20–22.

crucified (v. 2)—Though Paul expounded the whole counsel of God to the church (Acts 20:27) and taught the Corinthians the Word of God (Acts 18:11), the focus of his preaching and teaching to unbelievers was Jesus Christ, who paid the penalty for sin on the cross. Until someone understands and believes the gospel, there is nothing more to say to them. The preaching of the cross (1:18) was so dominant in the early church that believers were accused of worshiping a dead man.

weakness . . . fear . . . trembling (v. 3)—Paul came to Corinth after being beaten and imprisoned in Philippi, run out of Thessalonica and Berea, and scoffed at in Athens (Acts 16:22–24; 17:10, 13–14, 32), so he may have been physically weak. But in that weakness, he was most powerful (see vv. 4–5; 2 Cor. 12:9–10). There were no theatrics or techniques to manipulate people's response. His fear and shaking was because of the seriousness of his mission.

mature (v. 6)—Paul uses this word to refer to genuine believers who have been saved by Christ. The author of Hebrews uses a similar Greek word in this way in Hebrews 6:1; 10:14.

rulers (v. 6)—those in authority

this age (v. 6)—all periods of human history until the Lord returns

20 *and again, "The LORD knows the thoughts of the wise, that they are futile."*

21 *Therefore let no one boast in men. For all things are yours:*

22 *whether Paul or Apollos or Cephas, or the world or life or death, or things present or things to come—all are yours.*

23 *And you are Christ's, and Christ is God's.*

mystery (v. 7)—This term does not refer to something puzzling, but to truth known to God before time that He has kept secret until the appropriate time for Him to reveal it. (see Matt. 13:11 and Eph. 3:4–5).

for our glory (v. 7)—The truth God established before time and revealed in the New Testament wisdom of the gospel is the truth that God will save and glorify sinners. (see Eph. 3:8–12).

had they known (v. 8)—The crucifixion is proof that the rulers/Jewish religious leaders lacked wisdom. (see 1 Tim. 1:12–13).

as it is written (v. 9)—These words from Is. 64:4, often incorrectly thought to refer to the wonders of heaven, refer rather to the wisdom God has prepared for believers. God's truth is not discoverable by eye or ear (objective, empirical evidence), nor is it discovered by the mind (subjective, rational conclusions).

God has revealed them (v. 10) —By the Holy Spirit, God disclosed His saving truth. The Spirit alone was qualified because He knows all that God knows, Himself being God.

to us (v. 10)—As with the "we's" in verses 6–7 and verses 12–13, Paul is, first of all, speaking of himself and other apostles and, in a sense, of believers who have been given the Word as recorded by the apostles and their associates who wrote the New Testament.

we have received (v. 12)—The "we" and "us" refer to the apostles and other writers of the Word of God. The means was inspiration (see 2 Tim. 3:16; 2 Pet. 1:20–21), by which God freely gave the gift of His Word. It was this process of inspiration that turned the spiritual thoughts into spiritual words (v. 13) to give life (see Matt. 4:4).

natural man (v. 14)—This refers to the unconverted, who lack supernatural life and wisdom.

spiritually discerned (v. 14)— Through illumination of the Word, the Holy Spirit provides His saints the capacity to discern divine truth (see Ps. 119:18), which the spiritually dead are unable to comprehend (see John 5:37–39). The doctrine of illumination does not mean we know everything (see Deut. 29:29), that we do not need teachers (see Eph. 4:11–12), or that understanding does not require hard work (see 2 Tim. 2:15).

judged by no one (v. 15)—Obviously, unbelievers are able to recognize Christians' faults and shortcomings; but they are not able to evaluate their true nature as spiritual people who have been transformed into children of God (see 1 John 3:2).

the mind of Christ (v. 16)—Quoted from Is. 40:13. The same word is translated "understanding" in 14:14–15, 19. Believers are allowed, by the Word and the Spirit, to know the thoughts of their Lord. (see Luke 24:45).

carnal (v. 1)—Although Corinthian believers were no longer "natural," they were not "spiritual" (fully controlled by the Holy Spirit). In fact, they were "carnal" (controlled by the fallen flesh). Though all believers have the Holy Spirit, they still battle the fallen flesh (see Rom. 7:14–25).

babes in Christ (v. 1)–The carnality of those believers was indicative of their immaturity. They had no excuse for not being mature, since Paul implied that he should have been able to write to them as mature, in light of all he had taught them (v. 2).

milk (v. 2)–not a reference to certain doctrines, but to the more easily digestible truths of doctrine that were given to new believers

solid food (v. 2)—This refers to deeper features of the doctrines of Scripture. The difference is not in kind of truth, but degree of depth. Spiritual immaturity makes one unable to receive the richest truths.

envy, strife (v. 3)—Carnality produces the attitude of envy, a severe form of selfishness, which produces the action of strife and the subsequent divisions.

mere men (v. 3)—apart from the will of the Spirit, hence carnal, not spiritual

Paul . . . Apollos (v. 4)—Factionalism was the divisive product of carnality. (see 1:11–13).

Who then is Paul . . . Apollos (vv. 5–7)—a humble but accurate assessment of the roles that ministers play

the Lord gave . . . God gave . . . God who gives (vv. 5–7)—It is the Lord alone who can give faith to the spiritually ignorant and dead. Salvation is God's work of grace to whom He chooses to give it (see Eph. 2:8–9).

are one (v. 8)—All the human instruments God uses to produce salvation life are equally considered and rewarded for their willingness to be used by God. But all the glory goes to Him, who alone saves. Because of that, the silly favoritism of v. 4 and 1:12 is condemned.

we (v. 9)—Paul, Apollos, Peter, and all ministers are equal workers in the field, but the spiritual life from that field is entirely by God's grace and power.

God's building (v. 9)—Paul shifts the imagery from agricultural to construction (vv. 10–17).

master builder . . . foundation (v. 10)—The Greek word is the root for architect, but contained the idea of builder as well as designer. Paul's specialty was designing and building spiritual foundations. He was used by God to establish the groundwork for churches in Asia Minor, Macedonia, and Greece. Others (e.g., Timothy, Apollos) built the churches up from his foundations. That God used him in that way was all of grace (see v. 7; 15:20; Rom. 15:18).

each one (v. 10)—This primarily refers to evangelists and pastor-teachers.

no other foundation (v. 11)—Paul did not design the foundation; he only laid it by preaching Christ.

if anyone builds (v. 12)—This is, first of all, in reference to the evangelists and pastors (v. 9), and then to all believers who are called to build the church through faithful ministry.

gold, silver, precious stones (v. 12)—His quality materials represent dedicated spiritual service to build the church.

wood, hay, straw (v. 12)–These inferior materials imply shallow activity with no eternal value. They do not refer to activities that are evil (see note on v. 13).

the Day (v. 13)—refers to the time of the Judgment Seat of Christ

revealed by fire (v. 13)—the fire of God's discerning judgment (see Job 23;10; Zech. 13:9; 1 Pet. 1:17, 18; Rev. 3:18); 2 Corinthians 5:10 indicates that the wood, hay, and straw are "worthless" things that don't stand the test of judgment fire (see Col. 2:18)

endures (v. 14)—All that which has been accomplished in His power and for His glory will survive (see Matt. 25:21, 23; 2 Cor. 5:9; Phil. 3:13, 14; 2 Tim. 4:7, 8; James 1:12; 1 Pet. 5:4; Rev. 22:12).

reward (v. 14)—This is not a judgment for sin. Christ has paid that price (Rom. 8:1), so that no believer will ever be judged for sin. This is only to determine eternal reward (see 4:5, "each one's praise").

be saved (v. 15)—No matter how much is worthless, no believer will forfeit salvation.

deceive himself (vv. 18–19)—Those who defile the church and think they can succeed in destroying it by their human wisdom would do far better to reject that wisdom and accept the foolishness of Christ's cross.

boast in men (v. 21)—Cf. v. 4; 1:12. Paul, Apollos, and all others receive no credit for the building of the church.

all things are yours (v. 21)—All believers share equally in God's most important and valuable provisions and glories; human boasting, therefore, is ludicrous as well as sinful.

the world (v. 22)—Although the universe is now in Satan's grip, it is still the God-given and God-made possession of Christians (2 Cor. 4:15; 1 John 5:19). In the millennial kingdom and throughout eternity, however, believers will possess both the recreated and eternal earth in an infinitely more complete and rich way (Rev. 21).

life (v. 22)—spiritual, eternal life

death (v. 22)—spiritual and eternal death (15:54–57; Phil. 1:21–24)

things present (v. 22)—everything the believer has or experiences in this life

things to come (v. 22)—all the blessings of heaven; (see 1 Peter 1:3–4).

all are yours (v. 22)—In Christ, all good and holy things are for believers' blessing and for God's glory. (see Ephesians 1:3; 2 Peter 1:3).

Christ's . . . God's (v. 23)—Knowing that believers belong to Christ and therefore to each other is the greatest incentive for unity in the church (6:17; John 9:9–10, 21–23).

Understanding the Text

5) What specific situation was creating disharmony in the Corinthian church and why is unity so important for the church?

_____

_____

(verses to consider: John 17:11, 20–23; Acts 2:46–47; Rom. 12:5; Eph. 4:4–6)

6) Why did Paul say human wisdom is inadequate to meet the needs of the world?

_____

_____

(verses to consider: Is. 29:14; Rom. 1:18–23; James 3:13–18)

7) What was the centerpiece of Paul's message of foolishness (2:2)?

_____

_____

8) What role does the Holy Spirit play in bringing unity to God's people?

_____

_____

(verses to consider: Ezek. 36:25–27; John 14:26–27; 1 John 2:27)

Cross Reference

Read Romans 7:15–23.

15 *For what I am doing, I do not understand. For what I will to do, that I do not practice; but what I hate, that I do.*
16 *If, then, I do what I will not to do, I agree with the law that it is good.*
17 *But now, it is no longer I who do it, but sin that dwells in me.*
18 *For I know that in me (that is, in my flesh) nothing good dwells; for to will is present with me, but how to perform what is good I do not find.*
19 *For the good that I will to do, I do not do; but the evil I will not to do, that I practice.*
20 *Now if I do what I will not to do, it is no longer I who do it, but sin that dwells in me.*
21 *I find then a law, that evil is present with me, the one who wills to do good.*
22 *For I delight in the law of God according to the inward man.*

23 *But I see another law in my members, warring against the law of my mind, and bringing me into captivity to the law of sin which is in my members.*

Exploring the Meaning

9) How does this passage describe the Christian's battle with the flesh and carnal desires?

_____

_____

10) Read 2 Peter 1:5–13. What do these verses say is necessary for us to grow to maturity (and thus avoid being like the immature Corinthians)?

_____

_____

11) Read 2 Corinthians 5:10. How does (or how should) this promise of Christ's judgment of believers' works alter the way we live today?

_____

_____

(verses to consider: 1 Cor.4:5; 9:24–27; Rom. 14:10–12; Rev. 22:12)

Summing Up . . .

"When the Word of God is not set up as the supreme authority, division is inevitable. Such happens even in evangelical churches, when pastors and other leaders begin substituting their own ideas for the truths of Scripture. The substitution is seldom intentional, but it will always happen when the Bible is neglected. A Bible that is not studied carefully cannot be followed carefully. And where it is not followed there will be division, because there will be no common ground for beliefs and practices. When the truth of Scripture is not the sole authority, men's varied opinions become the authority."—*John MacArthur*

Reflecting on the Text

12) What are some things you need to do this week to help restore a damaged relationship with another Christian or group of Christians?

_____

_____

13) What spiritual disciplines (e.g., Bible study, Scripture memory and/or meditation, fasting, solitude, etc.) could you practice to make you more sensitive to the leading of God's Word and God's Spirit?

_____

_____

14) List some people in your life who are more impressed with the world's "wisdom" than with God's true wisdom, that is, the foolishness of the cross. How can you play a more active role this week in leading them to Christ?

_____

_____

Recording Your Thoughts

_____

_____

_____

For further study, see the following passages:

Isaiah 33:18	Matthew 5:5; 11:25	Matthew 12:38–44
Matthew 13:10–13	John 1:12;14:23	Acts 4:32; 17:21
Acts 26:16–18	Romans 8:9, 23	Romans 8:37–39
Romans 10:8–17	Romans 13:11;15:20	Romans 16:17
Ephesians 2:1–2	Ephesians 3:7–8	Ephesians 4:3
Philippians 1:27	Philippians 2:1–4	Col. 1:29
1 Thessalonians 2:19–20	Hebrews 5:12–14	1 Peter 1:3–4
1 Peter 2:6–8	Revelation 17:14	

True Servanthood

Opening Thought

1) If you were allowed to create the perfect pastor, what qualities would you build into this servant of God and why?

_____

_____

_____

2) What are the most obvious clues that a person is conceited? that a person is humble?

_____

_____

_____

3) What are the most common subjects of boasting or bragging in the church today?

_____

_____

_____

4) List the names of the folks who have had the greatest spiritual impact on you. List one or two outstanding qualities about each.

_____

_____

_____

Background of the Passage

Look at the manner in which the modern-day church (at least in the West) "picks" its spiritual leaders. Usually they are granted leadership status according to the size of their church or parachurch ministry. This celebrity status is enhanced if the person is on the speaker circuit—even more so if he/she has written popular books. The reputation grows if such a one is telegenic and entertaining. Effectiveness is often determined by the amount of revenue the "leader's" ministry takes in, by the number of TV stations airing the "leader's" program, by the number of crusades the "leader" undertakes.

All these things can be indicative of healthy, God-honoring ministry, but there are better, more reliable indicators. The New Testament advocates the concept of servant-leadership, a leadership style best embodied by Christ and best modeled in His willingness to humble himself and lay down His life for His followers.

Since the immature believers in Corinth were enamored (much as modern-day believers are) by "personalities," that is, high-profile Christian leaders, Paul took the opportunity in 1 Corinthians 4 to focus on the true nature and practice of godly servants. He emphasized the necessity of pure motives and genuine humility. Christ-honoring servants are not only identified as stewards (that is, managers) of the mysteries of God, but also as caring and committed spiritual fathers.

The picture presented by Paul is a far cry from the typical understanding of spiritual leadership. It is a picture most deserving of our attention and study.

Bible Passage

Read 1 Corinthians 4:1–21, noting the key words and definitions to the right of the passage.

1 Corinthians 4:1–21

1 Let a man so consider us, as servants of Christ and stewards of the mysteries of God.
2 Moreover it is required in stewards that one be found faithful.
3 But with me it is a very small thing that I should be judged by you or by a human court. In fact, I do not even judge myself.

so consider us (v. 1)—Paul wanted everyone to view him and his fellow ministers only as the humble messengers God ordained them to be (see 3:9, 22).

servants (v. 1)—Paul expresses his humility by using a word literally meaning "under rowers," referring to the lowest, most menial, and most despised galley slaves, who rowed on the bottom tier of a ship (9:16).

4 *For I know nothing against myself, yet I am not justified by this; but He who judges me is the Lord.*

5 *Therefore judge nothing before the time, until the Lord comes, who will both bring to light the hidden things of darkness and reveal the counsels of the hearts. Then each one's praise will come from God.*

6 *Now these things, brethren, I have figuratively transferred to myself and Apollos for your sakes, that you may learn in us not to think beyond what is written, that none of you may be puffed up on behalf of one against the other.*

7 *For who makes you differ from another? And what do you have that you did not receive? Now if you did indeed receive it, why do you boast as if you had not received it?*

8 *You are already full! You are already rich! You have reigned as kings without us—and indeed I could wish you did reign, that we also might reign with you!*

9 *For I think that God has displayed us, the apostles, last, as men condemned to death; for we have been made a spectacle to the world, both to angels and to men.*

10 *We are fools for Christ's sake, but you are wise in Christ! We are weak, but you are strong! You are distinguished, but we are dishonored!*

11 *To the present hour we both hunger and thirst, and we are poorly clothed, and beaten, and homeless.*

12 *And we labor, working with our own hands. Being reviled, we bless; being persecuted, we endure;*

13 *being defamed, we entreat. We have been made as the filth of the world, the offscouring of all things until now.*

14 *I do not write these things to shame you, but as my beloved children I warn you.*

15 *For though you might have ten thousand instruc-*

stewards. (v. 1)—Paul defines his responsibilities as an apostle by using a word originally referring to a person entrusted with and responsible for his master's entire household, e.g., buildings, fields, finances, food, other servants, and sometimes even children of the owner.

mysteries of God (v. 1)— "Mystery" is used in the New Testament to refer to divine revelation previously hidden. See notes on 2:7. Here the word is used in its broadest sense as God's full revealed truth in the New Testament (Acts 20:20–21, 27). As God's servant and steward, Paul had to oversee and dispense all scriptural truth.

faithful (v. 2)—The most essential quality of a servant or steward is obedient loyalty to his master (v. 17; 7:25).

human court (v. 3)—Paul is not being arrogant or saying that he is above fellow ministers, other Christians, or even certain unbelievers. He is saying that a human verdict on his life is not the one that matters, even if it is his own.

nothing against myself (v. 4) —Paul was not aware of any unconfessed or habitual sin in his own life, but his understanding was limited; his was not the final verdict.

not justified by this (v. 4)— Paul's own sincere evaluation of his life did not acquit him of all failures to be faithful.

the Lord (v. 4)—He is the ultimate and only qualified Judge of any man's obedience and faithfulness (2 Tim. 2:15). See also 2 Cor. 5:9–10.

hidden things of darkness . . . counsels of the hearts (v. 5) —These refer to the inner

tors in Christ, yet you do not have many fathers; for in Christ Jesus I have begotten you through the gospel.

16 Therefore I urge you, imitate me.

17 For this reason I have sent Timothy to you, who is my beloved and faithful son in the Lord, who will remind you of my ways in Christ, as I teach everywhere in every church.

18 Now some are puffed up, as though I were not coming to you.

19 But I will come to you shortly, if the Lord wills, and I will know, not the word of those who are puffed up, but the power.

20 For the kingdom of God is not in word but in power.

21 What do you want? Shall I come to you with a rod, or in love and a spirit of gentleness?

motives, thoughts, and attitudes which only God can know. Since final rewards will be based not only on outward service but also on inward devotion (see 10:31), only God can give the praise each deserves. See notes on 3:12–14.

these things (v. 6)—Paul is referring to the analogies he used to depict those who minister for the Lord, including himself and Apollos: farmers (3:6–9), builders (3:10–15), and servant-stewards (vv. 1–5).

your sakes (v. 6)—Paul's humility, expressed in light of God's judgment on the greatest apostles and preachers, was useful to teach believers not to exalt any of them (see Gen. 32:10; Judg. 6:15; John 1:26–27; Acts 20:19; 2 Cor. 3:5).

what is written (v. 6)— God's faithful servants are to be treated with respect only within the bounds of what is scriptural (1 Thess. 5:12; 1 Tim. 5:17).

puffed up (v. 6)—Pride and arrogance were great problems in the Corinthian church (see vv. 18–19; 5:2; 8:1; 13:4).

boast (v. 7)—Pride is deception, since everything a person possesses is from God's providential hand.

full . . . rich . . . reigned (v. 8) —In a severe rebuke, Paul heaps on false praise, sarcastically suggesting that those Corinthians who were self-satisfied had already achieved spiritual greatness. They were similar to the Laodiceans (see Rev. 3:17).

reign (v. 8)—Yet, Paul genuinely wished it really were the coronation time of the Millennium, so that they all might share in the glory of the Lord.

last (v. 9)—The imagery is of condemned prisoners brought into a Roman arena to fight and die; the last ones brought out for slaughter were the grand finale. In His sovereign wisdom and for His ultimate glory, God chose to display the apostles figuratively before men and angels during the present age as just such worthless and condemned spectacles (see Matt. 19:28). Like doomed gladiators, they were ridiculed, spit on, imprisoned, and beaten, yet God glorified His name through them as He used them to build His kingdom.

fools . . . wise (v. 10)—Again using sarcasm, this time on himself as if mimicking the attitude of the proud Corinthians toward him, Paul rebukes them.

the filth of the world (v. 13)—The apostles and early preachers lived at the lowest levels of society. While the Corinthians believers thought they were kings (v. 8), the apostle knew he was a suffering slave.

our own hands (v. 12)—The apostles did manual labor, which Greeks, including some in the church at Corinth, considered beneath their dignity and suitable only for slaves. But Paul was not resentful about any necessary labor needed to support gospel preaching (see Acts 18:3; 20:34).

filth . . . offscouring (v. 13)—This refers to the scum and dregs scraped from a dirty dish or garbage pot, figuratively used of the lowest, most degraded criminals, who were often sacrificed in pagan ceremonies. Paul and his fellow preachers were so designated—not in God's sight, but in the world's. What a rebuke of the proud, carnal Corinthians who saw themselves at the top, while the humble apostle considered himself at the bottom!

beloved children (v. 14)—Despite their carnal, even sometimes hateful immaturity, Paul always looked on the Corinthian believers with affection.

warn (v. 14)—literally, "put in mind," with the purpose of admonishing and reproving, presupposing that something is wrong and should be corrected (see Matt. 18:15–20; Acts 20:31)

ten thousand instructors (v. 15)—The terms actually say "countless tutors," referring by hyperbole to an unlimited number of moral guardians used with children. Only Paul was their spiritual father; hence, no one cared like him.

imitate me (v. 16)—See 11:1. The exhortation is bold, but justified. Spiritual leaders must set an example of Christlikeness for others to follow.

Timothy (v. 17)—He had been so faithfully discipled by Paul that he could be sent in the great apostle's place with confidence that he would perfectly represent him.

I teach (v. 17)—Referring to doctrine, not advice. By his own instruction and example, Timothy would reinforce the eternal truths Paul had taught him.

puffed up (vv. 18–19)—They were arrogant, thinking they would never have to face Paul again. But, if God allowed, he was planning to see them soon. He would not let their proud sinning go unchallenged, for their own sake as well as the gospel's. The reality of how much real spiritual power they had would become clear in that confrontation.

word . . . power (v. 20)—Spiritual character is measured not by the impressiveness of words but by the power of the life.

rod (v. 21)—Spiritual leaders need to use the rod of correction if people persist in sin. The pattern for that correction is illustrated and explained in 5:1–13.

Understanding the Text

5) What qualities did Paul say should mark a servant of Christ?

_____

_____

_____

(verses to consider: Matt. 24:45–51; 2 Cor.1:12; Titus 1:7–9)

6) What was the cause of the Corinthians' conceit and arrogance?

_____

_____

_____

7) How did Paul reveal a fatherly concern for the Corinthians?

_____

_____

_____

(verses to consider: 2 Cor.12:14–15; Gal. 4:19; 1 Thess. 2:4–12)

Cross Reference

Read 2 Corinthians 11:23–28.

²³ *Are they ministers of Christ?—I speak as a fool—I am more: in labors more abundant, in stripes above measure, in prisons more frequently, in deaths often.*

²⁴ *From the Jews five times I received forty stripes minus one.*

²⁵ *Three times I was beaten with rods; once I was stoned; three times I was shipwrecked; a night and a day I have been in the deep;*

²⁶ *in journeys often, in perils of waters, in perils of robbers, in perils of my own countrymen, in perils of the Gentiles, in perils in the city, in perils in the wilderness, in perils in the sea, in perils among false brethren;*

²⁷ *in weariness and toil, in sleeplessness often, in hunger and thirst, in fastings often, in cold and nakedness—*

²⁸ *besides the other things, what comes upon me daily: my deep concern for all the churches.*

Exploring the Meaning

8) How did Paul describe his life as an apostle?

_____

_____

(verses to consider: 2 Cor.1:8–9; 4:8–12; 1 Thess. 2:9; 2 Thess. 3:7–9)

9) Read 2 Corinthians 3:5. Why is humility so indispensable for God's people?

_____

_____

(verses to consider: Gen. 18:27; Ex. 3:11; Matt. 3:14; Luke 5:8; Eph. 3:8; Phil. 2:5–8; 1 Pet. 5:6)

10) Read Hebrews 13:17. What does this verse say is the proper way to respond to those who minister to and serve the church?

_____

_____

Summing Up . . .

"Many Christians have never become spiritual fathers. They have never produced any spiritual offspring. They have never led a person to Christ and helped train him in the ways of God. A Christian is one who has been given new life in Christ, and one of the most important characteristics of life is reproduction. Yet many believers have never reproduced believers. In a sense they are contradictions to what a Christian is. Every believer should be a spiritual father, God's instrument for bringing new lives into His kingdom."—*John MacArthur*

Reflecting on the Text

11) Which of Paul's character qualities do you most need to emulate today?

_____

_____

12) List three or four specific ways you can serve Christ by serving others today.

_____

_____

13) Do you see any areas of your life in which you are prideful or arrogant and in which you need the humility of Christ?

_____

_____

14) How can you show appreciation to your spiritual leaders this week?

_____

_____

Recording Your Thoughts

_____

_____

For further study, see the following passages:

1 Chronicles 29:11–16   Job 1:21   Matthew 7:21–23
Matthew 18:15–18   Luke 1:2   Acts 20:19
2 Corinthians 12:20   Ephesians 3:4–5   Philippians 3:12
Colossians 4:7   2 Timothy 2:2, 15   2 Timothy 3:10–14,16
2 Timothy 4:8   Hebrews 12:6; 13:7   James 1:12, 17
1 Peter 5:4

Immorality in the Church

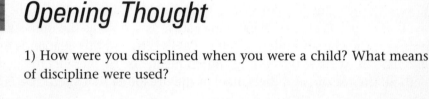

Opening Thought

1) How were you disciplined when you were a child? What means of discipline were used?

_____

_____

_____

2) Have you ever been part of a church that exercised discipline on sinning members? Why do you think most churches tend to shy away from such matters?

_____

_____

_____

3) What do you think is behind the popularity of television programs that focus on legal matters? Why is that an interesting subject to so many?

_____

_____

_____

4) To what degree can a court really solve disputes between two people or parties?

_____

_____

Background of the Passage

The city of Corinth in Paul's day was like much of Western society today. People were intent on having their own way. They wanted no restraints on their behavior, especially in regard to fulfilling physical lust. Sexual permissiveness was rampant; and then, as now, the church was not unaffected.

All of 1 Corinthians 5 is devoted to the problem of immorality in the church, much of it specifically to sexual immorality. As serious as the immorality itself, was the church's tolerance of it. Paul's thrust in this chapter is for the discipline of persistently sinning church members. He presents the need, the method, the reason, and the sphere of the discipline that should be imposed.

In chapter six, Paul first discusses and condemns the Corinthian tendency toward litigation. The members of the church had been so used to arguing, disputing, and taking one another to court before they were saved that they carried those selfish attitudes and habits over into their new lives as Christians. That course was not only spiritually wrong but also practically unnecessary.

Like many people today, the Corinthian Christians rationalized their sinful thinking and habits. They were clever at coming up with seemingly good reasons for doing wrong things. And so in 6:12–20, Paul returns to the issue of sexual sin and shows how it is at odds with the true freedom God intends for His people.

Bible Passage

Read 1 Corinthians 5:1–6:20, noting the key words and definitions to the right of the passage.

1 Corinthians 5:1–6:20

¹ It is actually reported that there is sexual immorality among you, and such sexual immorality as is not even named among the Gentiles—that a man has his father's wife!

² And you are puffed up, and have not rather mourned, that he who has done this deed might be taken away from among you.

sexual immorality (v. 1)— This sin was so vile that even the church's pagan neighbors were doubtless scandalized by it. The Corinthians had rationalized or minimized this sin, which was common knowledge, even though Paul had written them before about it (v. 9). The Greek for "immorality" is the root of the English word *pornography*.

3 For I indeed, as absent in body but present in spirit, have already judged (as though I were present) him who has so done this deed.

4 In the name of our Lord Jesus Christ, when you are gathered together, along with my spirit, with the power of our Lord Jesus Christ,

5 deliver such a one to Satan for the destruction of the flesh, that his spirit may be saved in the day of the Lord Jesus.

6 Your glorying is not good. Do you not know that a little leaven leavens the whole lump?

7 Therefore purge out the old leaven, that you may be a new lump, since you truly are unleavened. For indeed Christ, our Passover, was sacrificed for us.

8 Therefore let us keep the feast, not with old leaven, nor with the leaven of malice and wickedness, but with the unleavened bread of sincerity and truth.

9 I wrote to you in my epistle not to keep company with sexually immoral people.

10 Yet I certainly did not mean with the sexually immoral people of this world, or with the covetous, or extortioners, or idolaters, since then you would need to go out of the world.

11 But now I have written to you not to keep company with anyone named a brother, who is sexually immoral, or covetous, or an idolater, or a reviler, or a drunkard, or an extortioner—not even to eat with such a person.

12 For what have I to do with judging those also who are outside? Do you not judge those who are inside?

13 But those who are outside God judges. Therefore "put away from yourselves the evil person."

6:1 Dare any of you, having a matter against another, go to law before the unrighteous, and not before the saints?

2 Do you not know that the saints will judge the

---

his father's wife (v. 1)—This refers to the man's stepmother, with whom having sexual relations bore the same sinful stigma as if between him and his natural mother. Incest was punishable by death in the Old Testament (Lev. 18:29) and was both uncommon ("not even named") and illegal under Roman law.

puffed up (v. 2)—so arrogant and carnal as to excuse even that extreme wickedness

taken away (v. 2)—excommunicated as in verse 7

already judged (v. 3)—Paul had passed judgment on the sinner, and the church also needed to.

name of our Lord (v. 4)—consistent with His holy person and will

gathered together (v. 4)—This action is to be done when the church meets publicly.

power (v. 4)—Authority is in view. Action against unrepentant sinning in the church carries the weight of the Lord's authority.

deliver . . . to Satan (v. 5)— "Deliver" is a strong term, used of judicial sentencing. This is equal to excommunicating the professed believer. It amounts to putting that person out of the blessing of Christian worship and fellowship by thrusting him into Satan's realm, the world system.

the destruction of the flesh (v. 5)—This refers to divine chastening for sin that can result in illness and even death. (see notes on 11:29–32).

spirit . . . saved (v. 5)—The unrepentant person may suffer greatly under God's judgment but will not be an evil influence in the church; and he will more likely be saved under that judgment than if tolerated and accepted in the church.

world? And if the world will be judged by you, are you unworthy to judge the smallest matters?

3 Do you not know that we shall judge angels? How much more, things that pertain to this life?

4 If then you have judgments concerning things pertaining to this life, do you appoint those who are least esteemed by the church to judge?

5 I say this to your shame. Is it so, that there is not a wise man among you, not even one, who will be able to judge between his brethren?

6 But brother goes to law against brother, and that before unbelievers!

7 Now therefore, it is already an utter failure for you that you go to law against one another. Why do you not rather accept wrong? Why do you not rather let yourselves be cheated?

8 No, you yourselves do wrong and cheat, and you do these things to your brethren!

9 Do you not know that the unrighteous will not inherit the kingdom of God? Do not be deceived. Neither fornicators, nor idolaters, nor adulterers, nor homosexuals, nor sodomites,

10 nor thieves, nor covetous, nor drunkards, nor revilers, nor extortioners will inherit the kingdom of God.

11 And such were some of you. But you were washed, but you were sanctified, but you were justified in the name of the Lord Jesus and by the Spirit of our God.

12 All things are lawful for me, but all things are not helpful. All things are lawful for me, but I will not be brought under the power of any.

13 Foods for the stomach and the stomach for foods, but God will destroy both it and them. Now the body is not for sexual immorality but for the Lord, and the Lord for the body.

14 And God both raised up the Lord and will also raise us up by His power.

15 Do you not know that your bodies are members of Christ? Shall I then take the members of Christ

day of the Lord Jesus (v. 5)—This is the time when the Lord returns with His rewards for His people. (see note on 1:8).

glorying (v. 6)—Better, "boasting." It was not good, because their proud sense of satisfaction blinded them to their duty in regard to blatant sin that devastated the church.

leaven (v. 6)—In Scripture, it is used to represent influence, in most cases evil influence, although in Matt. 13:33 it refers to the good influence of the kingdom of heaven (see Ex. 13:3, 7).

whole lump (v. 6)—When tolerated, sin will permeate and corrupt the whole local church.

Christ, our Passover (v. 7)—Just as unleavened bread symbolized being freed from Egypt by the Passover, so the church is to be unleavened, since it has been separated from the dominion of sin and death by the perfect Passover Lamb, the Lord Jesus Christ. The church is, therefore, to remove everything sinful in order to be separate from the old life, including the influence of sinful church members.

keep the feast (v. 8)—In contrast to the Old Testament Passover feast celebrated annually, believers constantly celebrate the "feast" of the new Passover—Jesus Christ. As the Jews who celebrate Passover do so with unleavened bread, so believers celebrate their continual Passover with unleavened lives.

my epistle (v. 9)—A previous letter that Paul had written the church at Corinth instructed them to disassociate with the immoral (see v. 11).

people of this world (v. 10)—Evidently, the church had misinterpreted the advice in that letter and had stopped having contact with the unsaved in the world, while continuing to tolerate the sin of those in the church, which was even more dangerous to the fellowship. God

and make them members of a harlot? Certainly not!

16 Or do you not know that he who is joined to a harlot is one body with her? For "the two," He says, "shall become one flesh."

17 But he who is joined to the Lord is one spirit with Him.

18 Flee sexual immorality. Every sin that a man does is outside the body, but he who commits sexual immorality sins against his own body.

19 Or do you not know that your body is the temple of the Holy Spirit who is in you, whom you have from God, and you are not your own?

20 For you were bought at a price; therefore glorify God in your body and in your spirit, which are God's.

intends us to be in the world as witnesses.

named a brother (v. 11)—Paul clarifies his intention in the earlier letter. He expected them to disassociate with all who said they were brothers but had a consistent pattern of sin.

not even to eat (v. 11)—The meal was a sign of acceptance and fellowship in those days.

outside (vv. 12–13)—Paul never intended himself or the church to be judges of unbelievers outside the church, but to judge those inside. Those on the outside are for God to judge and believers to evangelize. Those who sin on the inside, the church is to put out.

Dare (6:1)—Suing another believer in a secular law court is a daring act of disobedience because of its implications related to all sin—the displeasure of God.

a matter against another (v. 1)—The phrase in Greek was commonly used of a lawsuit ("go to law").

unrighteous (v. 1)—This does not refer to their moral character but to their unsaved spiritual condition.

before the saints (v. 1)—Believers are to settle all issues between themselves within the church.

judge the world (v. 2)—Because Christians will assist Christ to judge the world in the millennial kingdom (Rev. 3:21), they are more than qualified with the truth, the Spirit, the gifts, and the resources they presently have in Him to settle small matters that come up among themselves in this present life.

judge angels (v. 3)—The Greek word can mean "rule" or "govern." Since the Lord Himself will judge fallen angels, it is likely this means we will have some rule in eternity over holy angels. Since angels are "ministering spirits" to serve the saints (Heb. 1:14), it seems reasonable that they will serve us in glory.

If then you have judgments (v. 3)—This is a difficult verse to translate, as suggested by the widely varying English renderings. However, the basic meaning is clear: When Christians have earthly quarrels and disputes among themselves, it is inconceivable that they would turn to those least qualified (unbelievers) to resolve the matter. The most legally untrained believers, who know the Word of God and are obedient to the Spirit, are far more competent to settle disagreements between believers than the most experienced unbeliever, void of God's truth and Spirit.

shame (vv. 5–6)—Such conduct as suing a fellow believer is not only a sinful shame (v. 5), but a complete failure to act obediently and righteously. Christians who take fellow Christians to court suffer moral defeat and spiritual loss even before the case is heard, and they become subject to divine chastening (see Heb. 12:3ff.).

Why . . . not . . . accept wrong? (v. 7)—The implied answer is that the Corinthians are not willing to be wronged because of their shameful sin (v. 5) and the moral defeat (v. 8) that result from selfishness and their willingness to discredit God, His wisdom, power, and sovereign purpose, and to harm the church and the testimony of Christ's gospel.

cheated (v. 7)—Christians have no right to insist on legal recourse in a public court. It is far better to trust God's sovereign purposes in trouble and lose financially than to be disobedient and suffer spiritually (see notes on Matt. 5:39–40; 18:21–35).

you yourselves do wrong and cheat (v. 8)—He is referring to those who sue their brothers in Christ as being guilty of the same misconduct they are suing to rectify.

Neither fornicators, nor idolaters . . . (vv. 9–10)—This catalog of sins, though not exhaustive, represents the major types of moral sin that characterize the unsaved.

not inherit the kingdom (v. 9)—The kingdom is the spiritual sphere of salvation where God rules as king over all who belong to Him by faith. All believers are in that spiritual kingdom, yet are waiting to enter into the full inheritance of it in the age to come. People who are characterized by these iniquities are not saved (v. 10). While believers can and do commit these sins, they do not characterize them as an unbroken life pattern. When they do, it demonstrates that the person is not in God's kingdom. True believers who do sin, resent that sin and seek to gain the victory over it.

fornicators (v. 9)—all who indulge in sexual immorality, but particularly unmarried persons

idolaters (v. 9)—those who worship any false god or follow any false religious system

adulterers (v. 9)—married persons who indulge in sexual acts outside their marriage

homosexuals . . . sodomites (v. 9)—These terms refer to those who exchange and corrupt normal male-female sexual roles and relations. Transvestism, sex changes, and other gender perversions are included (see Gen. 1:27). Sodomites are so called because the sin of male-male sex dominated the city of Sodom (Gen. 18:20) This sinful perversion is condemned always, in any form, by Scripture (see Lev. 18:22; Rom. 1:26, 27).

thieves . . . covetous (v. 10)—Both are guilty of the same basic sin of greed. Those who are covetous desire what belongs to others; thieves actually take it.

revilers (v. 10)—people who try to destroy others with words

extortioners (v. 10)—swindlers and embezzlers who steal indirectly, taking unfair advantage of others for their own financial gain

some of you (v. 11)—Though not all Christians have been guilty of all those particular sins, every Christian is equally an ex-sinner, since Christ came to save sinners (see Matt. 9:13). Some who used to have those patterns of sinful life were falling into those old sins again and needed reminding that if they went all the way back to live as they used to, they were not going to inherit eternal salvation, because it would indicate that they never were saved (see 2 Cor. 5:17).

washed (v. 11)—refers to new life, through spiritual cleansing and regeneration (see John 3:3–8; 2 Cor. 5:17)

sanctified (v. 11)—This results in new behavior, which a transformed life always produces. Sin's total domination is broken and replaced by a new pattern of obedience and holiness. Though not perfection, this is a new direction (see Rom. 6:17–18, 22).

justified (v. 11)—This refers to a new standing before God, in which the Christian is clothed in Christ's righteousness. In His death, the believer's sins were put to His account and He suffered for them, so that His righteousness might be put to an account, so that we might be blessed for it (Rom. 3:26; 4:22–25; 2 Cor. 5:21; Phil. 3:8–9; 1 Pet. 3:18).

by the Spirit (v. 11)—The Holy Spirit is the agent of salvation's transformation (see John 3:3–5).

All things are lawful . . . not helpful (v. 12)—"All things are lawful" may have been a Corinthian slogan. It was true that no matter what sins a believer commits, God forgives (Eph. 1:7), but not everything is profitable or beneficial. The price of abusing freedom and grace is very high. Sin always produces loss.

power (v. 12)—Sin has power. The word means "mastered" (see Rom. 6:14), and no sin is more enslaving than sexual sin. While it can never be the unbroken pattern of a true believer's life, it can be the recurring habit that saps joy, peace, and usefulness, and brings divine chastening and even church discipline (see 5:1ff.). Sexual sin controls, so the believer must never allow sin to have that control but must master it in the Lord's strength (see note on 9:27). Paul categorically rejects the ungodly notion that freedom in Christ gives license to sin (see Rom. 7:6; 8:13, 21).

Foods . . . stomach (v. 13)—Perhaps this was a popular proverb to celebrate the idea that sex is purely biological, like eating. The influence of philosophical dualism may have contributed to this idea since it made only the body evil; therefore, what one did physically was not preventable and was thus inconsequential. Because the relationship between these two is purely biological and temporal, the Corinthians, like many of their pagan friends, probably used that analogy to justify sexual immorality.

the body . . . the Lord (v. 13)—Paul rejects the convenient justifying analogy. Bodies and food are temporal relations that will perish.

members (v. 15)—The believer's body is not only for the Lord here and now (v. 14) but is of the Lord, a part of His body, the church (Eph. 1:22–23). The Christian's body is a spiritual temple in which the Spirit of Christ lives (12:3; John 7:38–39; 20:22; Acts 1:8; Rom. 8:9); therefore, when a believer commits a sexual sin, it involves Christ with a harlot. All sexual sin is harlotry.

Certainly not! (v. 15)—These words translate the strongest Greek negative— "may it never be so."

one flesh (v. 16)—Paul supports his point in the previous verse by appealing to Genesis 2:24 which defines the sexual union between a man and a woman as "one flesh." When a person is joined to a harlot, it is a one-flesh experience; therefore Christ spiritually is joined to that harlot.

one spirit with Him (v. 17)—Further strengthening the point, Paul affirms that all sex outside of marriage is sin; but illicit relationships by believers are especially reprehensible because they profane Jesus Christ, with whom believers are one (John 15:4, 7; 17:20–23). This argument should make such sin unthinkable.

Every sin . . . is outside (v. 18)—There is a sense in which sexual sin destroys a person like no other, because it is so intimate and entangling, corrupting on the deepest human level. But Paul is probably alluding to venereal disease, prevalent and devastating in his day and today. No sin has greater potential to destroy the body, something a believer should avoid because of the reality given in verses 19–20.

not your own (v. 19)—A Christian's body belongs to the Lord (v. 13), is a member of Christ (v. 15), and is the Holy Spirit's temple. Every act of fornication, adultery, or any other sin is committed by the believer in the sanctuary, the Holy of Holies, where God dwells. In the Old Testament, the High Priest went in there only once a year, and only after extensive cleansing, lest he be killed (Lev. 16).

a price (v. 20)—the precious blood of Christ (see 1 Pet. 1:18–19)

glorify God (v. 20)—the Christian's supreme purpose (10:31)

Understanding the Text

5) What precise immoral situation were the Corinthians allowing and why?

_____

6) What was Paul's apostolic command to the church regarding this sinning brother?

_____

(verses to consider: Matt. 18:15–18; Eph. 5:3; 2 Thess. 3:6)

7) According to Paul, whom should the church hold to a higher standard: believers or unbelievers? Why?

_____

(verses to consider: Matt. 5:13–16; Acts 1:8; Phil. 2:14–16)

Cross Reference

Read 2 Thessalonians 3:6–15.

⁶ *But we command you, brethren, in the name of our Lord Jesus Christ, that you withdraw from every brother who walks disorderly and not according to the tradition which he received from us.*

⁷ *For you yourselves know how you ought to follow us, for we were not disorderly among you;*

⁸ *nor did we eat anyone's bread free of charge, but worked with labor and toil night and day, that we might not be a burden to any of you,*

⁹ *not because we do not have authority, but to make ourselves an example of how you should follow us.*

¹⁰ *For even when we were with you, we commanded you this: If anyone will not work, neither shall he eat.*

¹¹ *For we hear that there are some who walk among you in a disorderly manner,*

not working at all, but are busybodies.

¹² *Now those who are such we command and exhort through our Lord Jesus Christ that they work in quietness and eat their own bread.*

¹³ *But as for you, brethren, do not grow weary in doing good.*

¹⁴ *And if anyone does not obey our word in this epistle, note that person and do not keep company with him, that he may be ashamed.*

¹⁵ *Yet do not count him as an enemy, but admonish him as a brother.*

Exploring the Meaning

8) What additional insight does this passage shed on the New Testament practice of church discipline?

_____

_____

(verses to consider: Gal. 6:1–2; Prov. 27:6)

9) Read Matt. 5:39–40. Compare this teaching of Christ with Paul's counsel regarding lawsuits between believers.

_____

_____

(verses to consider: 1 John 3:10–11; Matt. 18:21–35)

10) Read Galatians 5:13. How can Christians "lose" their freedom if they are not careful? How can sexual temptation and sin be especially enslaving?

_____

_____

(verses to consider: Gal. 5:1; Rom. 6:1; 7:6; 8:21; Prov. 5:3–19; 1 Thess. 4:3–5)

Summing Up . . .

"It is not that everyone in the church must be perfect, for that is impossible. Everyone falls into sin and has imperfections and shortcomings. The church is in some ways a hospital for those who know they are sick. They have trusted in Christ as Savior and they want to follow Him as Lord—to be what God wants them to be. It is not the ones who recognize their sin and hunger for righteousness who are to be put out of fellowship, but those who persistently and unrepentantly continue in a pattern of sin about which they have been counseled and warned. We should continue to love them and pray for them that they repent and return to a pure life. If they do repent we should gladly and joyfully 'forgive and comfort' them and welcome them back into fellowship (2 Cor. 2:7)."—*John MacArthur*

Reflecting on the Text

11) What safeguards can you put in place to keep you from becoming callous to sins among the people of God?

_____

12) What truths from this lesson do you need to remember next time you are wronged by a fellow believer?

_____

13) Anticipate your schedule over the next couple of weeks. In what specific situations do you especially need to remember that "you are not your own . . . for you were bought at a price"?

_____

Recording Your Thoughts

_____

For further study, see the following passages:

Genesis 19:4–5	Exodus 12:16–17	Leviticus 18:7–8
Leviticus 20:13	Deuteronomy 17:7; 22:5	Deuteronomy 22:30
Daniel 7:22	Mark 8:15	John 14:18–23
Acts 2:32; 5:1–11	Romans 5:20; 7:14–25	Romans 12:1–2; 12:5
2 Corinthians 6:16	Ephesians 2:10	Philippians 3:20–21
1 Timothy 1:10	Titus 3:5	1 Peter 4:17
2 Peter 2:4	1 John 3:9–10	Jude 6
Revelation 2:26–27		

Marriage in the Church

Opening Thought

1) What would you say are the top seven components of a good, healthy, God-honoring marriage? Why?

_____

_____

_____

_____

_____

2) What couple or couples do you most admire for the way they interact as husband and wife? Just what about them do you admire?

_____

_____

_____

_____

_____

3) What are the pluses and minuses (in contemporary culture) of being single?

_____

_____

_____

_____

Background of the Passage

In the United States today about every other marriage ends in divorce. There are nearly as many divorces as marriages each year. Love today is loudly acclaimed and sought after, but it is not much evident—even within marriages.

Marriage problems are not unique to modern times. They have occurred throughout history and were rampant in New Testament times in the Roman empire. As with their many other problems, much of the marital difficulty that permeated the Corinthian church reflected the pagan and morally corrupt society in which they lived and from which they had not fully separated.

In chapter 7, obviously answering a question or questions posed by confused, discontented Corinthian believers, Paul addresses the issues of marriage and singleness. Some wanted to change their marital status, some were slaves who wanted to be free, and some used their freedom in Christ to rationalize sinning. In a general response to that, Paul plainly repeats the basic principle that Christians should willingly accept the marital condition and social situations into which God has placed them and be content to serve Him there until He leads them elsewhere.

He teaches that marriage is the norm for Christians. He also gives the most comprehensive teaching in all of Scripture on the subject of singleness. In short, he maintains that celibacy is good, that it can be tempting, that it is wrong for married people, that it is a gift from God, but that it is not superior to marriage.

This chapter gives guidelines—wise counsel and comfort—for Christians married to Christians as well as for believers married to unbelievers. It calls for lifelong marriage relationships.

First Corinthians 7, studied and heeded, is the perfect antidote to the distressing state of marriage in these days. It is a chapter worthy of our close attention.

Bible Passage

Read 1 Corinthians 7:1–40, noting the key words and definitions to the right of the passage.

1 Corinthians 7:1–40

¹ Now concerning the things of which you wrote to me: It is good for a man not to touch a woman.

It is good (vv. 1–7)—Some had the notion that because of all the sexual sin and marital confusion, it would be even more spiritual to be celibate. This could lead some false-

² *Nevertheless, because of sexual immorality, let each man have his own wife, and let each woman have her own husband.*

³ *Let the husband render to his wife the affection due her, and likewise also the wife to her husband.*

⁴ *The wife does not have authority over her own body, but the husband does. And likewise the husband does not have authority over his own body, but the wife does.*

⁵ *Do not deprive one another except with consent for a time, that you may give yourselves to fasting and prayer; and come together again so that Satan does not tempt you because of your lack of self-control.*

⁶ *But I say this as a concession, not as a commandment.*

⁷ *For I wish that all men were even as I myself. But each one has his own gift from God, one in this manner and another in that.*

⁸ *But I say to the unmarried and to the widows: It is good for them if they remain even as I am;*

⁹ *but if they cannot exercise self-control, let them marry. For it is better to marry than to burn with passion.*

¹⁰ *Now to the married I command, yet not I but the Lord: A wife is not to depart from her husband.*

¹¹ *But even if she does depart, let her remain unmarried or be reconciled to her husband. And a husband is not to divorce his wife.*

¹² *But to the rest I, not the Lord, say: If any brother has a wife who does not believe, and she is willing to live with him, let him not divorce her.*

¹³ *And a woman who has a husband who does not believe, if he is willing to live with her, let her not divorce him.*

¹⁴ *For the unbelieving husband is sanctified by the wife, and the unbelieving wife is sanctified by the husband; otherwise your children would be unclean, but now they are holy.*

---

ly pious people to advocate divorce in order to be single. These verses elevate singleness, as long as it is celibate, but they in no way teach that marriage is either wrong or inferior.

touch a woman (v. 1)—This is a Jewish euphemism for sexual intercourse (see Ruth 2:9). Paul is saying that it is good not to have sex, that is, to be single and celibate. It is not, however, the only good or even better than marriage.

sexual immorality (v. 2)—There is a great danger of sexual sin when single. Marriage is God's only provision for sexual fulfillment. Marriage should not be reduced simply to that, however. Paul has a much higher view and articulates it in Ephesians 5:22–23. Here he is stressing the issue of sexual sin for people who are single.

render . . . affection due (v. 3)—Married believers are not to sexually deprive their spouses. While celibacy is right for the single, it is wrong for the married. The practice of deprivation may have been most common when a believer had an unsaved spouse (for more on unsaved spouses, see notes on vv. 10–17).

authority (v. 4)—By the marriage covenant, each partner is given the right over the spouse's body for the satisfaction of the other.

deprive (v. 5)—Literally this says, "Stop depriving each other!" This command may indicate that this kind of deprivation was going on among believers, perhaps in reaction to the gross sexual sins of their past. Husbands and wives may abstain temporarily from sexual activity, but only when they mutually agree to do so for intercession, as a part of their fasting.

come together again (v. 5)—Sexual intercourse is to be renewed soon after the spiritual interruption.

¹⁵ *But if the unbeliever departs, let him depart; a brother or a sister is not under bondage in such cases. But God has called us to peace.*

¹⁶ *For how do you know, O wife, whether you will save your husband? Or how do you know, O husband, whether you will save your wife?*

¹⁷ *But as God has distributed to each one, as the Lord has called each one, so let him walk. And so I ordain in all the churches.*

¹⁸ *Was anyone called while circumcised? Let him not become uncircumcised. Was anyone called while uncircumcised? Let him not be circumcised.*

¹⁹ *Circumcision is nothing and uncircumcision is nothing, but keeping the commandments of God is what matters.*

²⁰ *Let each one remain in the same calling in which he was called.*

²¹ *Were you called while a slave? Do not be concerned about it; but if you can be made free, rather use it.*

²² *For he who is called in the Lord while a slave is the Lord's freedman. Likewise he who is called while free is Christ's slave.*

²³ *You were bought at a price; do not become slaves of men.*

²⁴ *Brethren, let each one remain with God in that state in which he was called.*

²⁵ *Now concerning virgins: I have no commandment from the Lord; yet I give judgment as one whom the Lord in His mercy has made trustworthy.*

²⁶ *I suppose therefore that this is good because of the present distress—that it is good for a man to remain as he is:*

²⁷ *Are you bound to a wife? Do not seek to be loosed. Are you loosed from a wife? Do not seek a wife.*

²⁸ *But even if you do marry, you have not sinned; and if a virgin marries, she has not sinned. Nevertheless such will have trouble in the flesh, but I would spare you.*

so that Satan does not tempt (v. 5)—After the agreed-upon time of abstinence, sexual desires intensify and a spouse becomes more vulnerable to sinful desire.

concession (v. 6)—A better translation of the Greek would be "awareness" or "to have a mutual opinion." Paul was very aware of the God-ordained advantages of both singleness and marriage, and was not commanding marriage because of the temptations of singleness. Spirituality is not connected at all to marital status, though marriage is God's good gift (see 1 Pet. 3:7, "the grace of life").

as I myself (v. 7)—As a single person, Paul recognized the special freedom and independence he had to serve Christ (see notes on vv. 32–34). But he did not expect all believers to be single, nor all who were single to stay that way, nor all who were married to be celibate as if they were single.

gift from God (v. 7)—Both singleness and marriage are God's gracious gifts.

unmarried . . . widows (v. 8)—"Unmarried" is a term used four times in the New Testament, and only in 1 Corinthians (see vv. 11, 32, 34). This verse makes it clear that the unmarried and widows are distinct. Verse 11 identifies the divorced as the "unmarried" to be distinguished from "widows" (vv. 39–40; single by death) and virgins (vv. 25, 28; never married). Each use of "unmarried," then, refers to those formerly married, presently single, but not widowed. They are the divorced. It is likely these people who were formerly married wanted to know if they, as Christians, could or should remarry.

as I am (v. 8)—Paul was possibly a widower and could here affirm his former marriage by identifying with the unmarried and widows. His first suggestion is that they stay single because of its freedoms in serving the Lord (vv. 25–27, 32–34).

²⁹ *But this I say, brethren, the time is short, so that from now on even those who have wives should be as though they had none,*

³⁰ *those who weep as though they did not weep, those who rejoice as though they did not rejoice, those who buy as though they did not possess,*

³¹ *and those who use this world as not misusing it. For the form of this world is passing away.*

³² *But I want you to be without care. He who is unmarried cares for the things of the Lord—how he may please the Lord.*

³³ *But he who is married cares about the things of the world—how he may please his wife.*

³⁴ *There is a difference between a wife and a virgin. The unmarried woman cares about the things of the Lord, that she may be holy both in body and in spirit. But she who is married cares about the things of the world—how she may please her husband.*

³⁵ *And this I say for your own profit, not that I may put a leash on you, but for what is proper, and that you may serve the Lord without distraction.*

³⁶ *But if any man thinks he is behaving improperly toward his virgin, if she is past the flower of youth, and thus it must be, let him do what he wishes. He does not sin; let them marry.*

³⁷ *Nevertheless he who stands steadfast in his heart, having no necessity, but has power over his own will, and has so determined in his heart that he will keep his virgin, does well.*

³⁸ *So then he who gives her in marriage does well, but he who does not give her in marriage does better.*

³⁹ *A wife is bound by law as long as her husband lives; but if her husband dies, she is at liberty to be married to whom she wishes, only in the Lord.*

⁴⁰ *But she is happier if she remains as she is, according to my judgment—and I think I also have the Spirit of God.*

let them marry (v. 9)—The Greek tense indicates a command, since a person can't live a happy life and serve the Lord effectively if dominated by unfulfilled sexual passion—especially in that Corinthian society.

not I but the Lord (v. 10)—What Paul writes to these believers was already made clear by Jesus during His earthly ministry (Matt. 19:5–8; see Gen. 2:24).

depart (v. 10)—This word is used as a synonym for divorce, as indicated by the parallel use of the word "divorce" in verse 11. Apparently, some Christians felt they should divorce their unsaved spouses, to live celibately or marry a believer.

remain unmarried (v. 11)—If a Christian divorces another Christian except for adultery (see Matt. 5:31–32), neither partner is free to marry another person. They should reconcile, or at least remain unmarried.

to the rest (v. 12)—Those not covered by the instruction of verses 10–11.

I . . . say (v. 12)—Not a denial of inspiration or an indication that Paul is giving human opinion, but simply a way of saying that Jesus had not spoken on this and God had not previously given revelation on the matter.

sanctified (v. 14)—This does not refer to salvation; otherwise the spouse would not be spoken of as unbelieving. The sanctification is matrimonial and familial, not personal or spiritual, and means that the unsaved partner is set apart for temporal blessing because the other belongs to God. One Christian in a marriage brings grace that spills over on the spouse—even possibly leading them to salvation.

children . . . are holy (v. 14)—The Christian need not separate from an unbeliever because of fear that the unbelieving spouse may defile the children. God promises the opposite. They would be unclean if both parents were unsaved, but the presence of one believing parent exposes the children to blessing and brings them protection. The presence of even one Christian parent will protect children from undue spiritual harm, and they will receive many blessings, often including salvation.

let him depart (v. 15)—A term referring to divorce (see vv. 10–11). When an unbelieving spouse cannot tolerate the partner's faith and wants a divorce, it is best to let that happen in order to preserve peace in the family (see Rom. 12:18). The bond of marriage is broken only by death (Rom. 7:2), adultery (Matt. 19:9), or an unbeliever's leaving.

not under bondage (v. 15)—When the bond is broken in any of those ways, a Christian is free to marry another believer. Throughout Scripture, whenever legitimate divorce occurs, remarriage is assumed. When divorce is permitted, so is remarriage. By implication, the permission for a widow to remarry (vv. 39–40; Rom. 7:3), because the "bond" is broken, extends to this case, where there is no more "bondage."

how do you know (v. 16)—Some may have been reluctant to let go of their unsaved spouse, who wanted out and was creating discord in the home—thinking they could evangelize the spouse by hanging on for the purpose of seeing that one converted. Paul says there are no such assurances and it is better to divorce and be at peace (v. 15), if the unsaved partner wants to end the marriage that way.

called (v. 18)—As always in the epistles, this term refers to God's effectual call that saves.

circumcised . . . uncircumcised (v. 18)—With Judaizers demanding all Gentile believers in Christ be circumcised (Gal. 5:1–6), and with some Christian Jews wanting to disassociate with Judaism and thus having a surgery to become uncircumcised (as addressed in rabbinic literature), Paul needed to clarify the issue by saying that neither was necessary. Figuratively, the idea is that when a Jew became a Christian, he was not to give up his racial and cultural identity in order to appear like a Gentile. Likewise, a Gentile was not to become culturally like a Jew (v. 19). Culture, social order, and external ceremony have no bearing on spiritual life. What matters is faith and obedience.

while a slave (v. 21)—Paul was not approving all slavery but is teaching that a person who is a slave is still able to obey and honor Christ (Eph. 6:5–8).

Do not be concerned about (v. 21)—In modern society, this seems an insensitive command to those who wrongly assume that freedom is some God-given right rather than a preferable option.

the Lord's freedman (v. 22)—In the ways that truly count, no man is freer than a Christian. No bondage is as terrible as that of sin, from which Christ frees the believer.

Christ's slave (v. 22)—Those who are not slaves, but free in the social sense, are in the spiritual sense made slaves of Christ in salvation (Rom. 6:22).

price (v. 23)—the blood of Christ (6:20; 1 Pet. 1:19)

slaves of men (v. 23)—This refers to sinful slavery, that is, becoming slaves to the ways of men, the ways of the world, and of the flesh. This is the slavery about which to be concerned.

I have no commandment (v. 25)—See note on v. 12. The conviction given here is not a command, but is thoroughly dependable and sound advice to remain a virgin, which is counsel included by the inspiration of the Spirit from a trustworthy man.

present distress (v. 26)—an unspecified, current calamity; perhaps Paul anticipated the imminent Roman persecutions which began within ten years after this epistle was written

remain as he is (v. 26)—Persecution is difficult enough for a single person to endure, but problems and pain are multiplied for those who are married, especially if they have children.

loosed (v. 27)—Divorce is in view.

marry, you have not sinned (v. 28)—Marriage is a fully legitimate and godly option for both the divorced (on biblical grounds; see note on v. 15) and virgins.

trouble in the flesh (v. 28)—"Trouble" means literally "pressed together, or under pressure." Marriage can involve conflicts, demands, difficulties, and adjustments that singleness does not, because it presses two fallen people into intimate life that leads to inevitable "trouble." The troubles of singleness may be exceeded by the conflicts of marriage.

time is short (v. 29)—Human life is brief (see 1 Pet. 1:24).

as though they had none (v. 29)—This does not teach that marriage is no longer binding or treated with seriousness, nor should there be any physical deprivation (vv. 3–5); but Paul is teaching that marriage should not at all reduce one's devotion to the Lord and service to Him (see Col. 3:2). He means to keep the eternal priority (see v. 31).

use . . . not misusing (v. 31)—This refers to the normal commercial materialism and pleasures that govern in the world. Believers are not to be swept up in earthly enterprises so that heavenly matters become secondary.

form (v. 31)—This refers to a manner of life, a fashion, or way of doing things.

be without care (vv. 32–33)—A single person is free from concern about the earthly needs of a spouse and therefore potentially better able to set himself apart exclusively for the Lord's work.

things of the world (v. 33)—These are earthly matters connected to the passing system (v. 31).

how he may please his wife . . . husband (vv. 33–34)—Here is a basic and expected principle for a good marriage—each seeking to please the other.

There is a difference between a wife and a virgin (v. 34)—The first part of this verse is preferably rendered in some manuscripts, "and his interests are divided. And the woman who is unmarried and the virgin . . . ." This is important because it distinguishes clearly between the "unmarried" and "virgins," who, therefore, can't be the same. "Virgins" are single people never married, while "unmarried" must be single by divorce. *Widows* is the term for those made single by death (see note on v. 8).

distraction (v. 35)—See notes on verses 26, 29, 33.

his virgin (v. 36)—That is, a man's daughter. Apparently in Corinth some of the fathers, intending devotion to the Lord, had dedicated their young daughters to the Lord as permanent virgins.

past the flower of youth (v. 36)—fully matured as a woman capable of child bearing

it must be (v. 36)—When daughters became of marriageable age and insisted on being married, their fathers were free to let them marry.

no necessity (v. 37)—This means the father who has kept his daughter a virgin and is not under constraint by the daughter to change his mind, does well to fulfill his desire for her to be singularly devoted to the Lord (v. 34). As with those who remain single (v. 28), the choice was not between right and wrong.

bound by law (v. 39)—God's law designed marriage for life. It is so permanent that the disciples thought it might be better not to marry (see Matt. 19:10).

only in the Lord (v. 39)—that is, free to marry a believer only; this is true for all believers who marry or remarry

I also have the Spirit (v. 41)—Perhaps with a touch of sarcasm, Paul affirmed that this sound advice was given by the Holy Spirit.

Understanding the Text

4) What broad truths about marriage does Paul teach in this chapter? About celibacy?

_____

_____

_____

(verses to consider: Gen. 1:28; 2:18; Matt. 19:12)

5) What specific instructions does Paul give here to those who are married?

_____

_____

_____

6) What precise instructions does Paul give here to those who are single?

_____

_____

_____

7) What advantages do single people have over those who are married?

_____

_____

_____

Cross Reference

Read Ephesians 5:22–33.

²² *Wives, submit to your own husbands, as to the Lord.*
²³ *For the husband is head of the wife, as also Christ is head of the church; and He is the Savior of the body.*

24 *Therefore, just as the church is subject to Christ, so let the wives be to their own husbands in everything.*

25 *Husbands, love your wives, just as Christ also loved the church and gave Himself for her,*

26 *that He might sanctify and cleanse her with the washing of water by the word,*

27 *that He might present her to Himself a glorious church, not having spot or wrinkle or any such thing, but that she should be holy and without blemish.*

28 *So husbands ought to love their own wives as their own bodies; he who loves his wife loves himself.*

29 *For no one ever hated his own flesh, but nourishes and cherishes it, just as the Lord does the church.*

30 *For we are members of His body, of His flesh and of His bones.*

31 *"For this reason a man shall leave his father and mother and be joined to his wife, and the two shall become one flesh."*

32 *This is a great mystery, but I speak concerning Christ and the church.*

33 *Nevertheless let each one of you in particular so love his own wife as himself, and let the wife see that she respects her husband.*

Exploring the Meaning

8) What extra insights does this familiar passage shed on the grandeur and purpose of Christian marriage?

_____

_____

9) Read 1 Corinthians 10:13. How does the promise of this verse apply to the specific situations faced by both married and single persons?

_____

_____

10) Read Malachi 2:16. What does this passage teach about God's design for marriage?

_____

_____

(verses to consider: Matt. 5:31–32; 19:3–6)

Summing Up . . .

"Marriage was instituted by God and is the norm for man-woman relationships, and it is a great blessing to mankind. But it is not required for believers or for anyone else. His point was: If you are single that is good, and if you are married or get married, stay married and retain normal marital relations, for that is of God. Spirituality is not determined by marital status."—*John MacArthur*

Reflecting on the Text

11) Which part(s) of this study on marriage and singleness do you find most encouraging? Most convicting?

12) How should the reminder that life is brief (v. 29) affect your priorities and decisions today?

13) Single or married, what God-honoring steps can you take this week to become less focused on the things of earth and more concerned with eternal matters?

14) How can you use your unique station in life (married or not) today to serve and honor God?

Recording Your Thoughts

For further study, see the following passages:

Matthew 5:31–32	Matthew 19:8–9	Luke 2:36–38
2 Corinthians 6:14–16	Colossians 3:18–19	Colossians 3:23
1 Timothy 6:1–2	James 4:14	

The Limits of Christian Liberty

1 Corinthians 8:1–11:1

Opening Thought

1) When (if ever) in your life have you had disagreements with other Christians over the appropriateness of certain behaviors that are not clearly discussed or forbidden by Scripture? Have you ever participated in a "questionable" activity and later felt regret at having done so? Why did you regret it?

_____

_____

_____

2) How can and should history (that is, the good and bad experiences of those who have come before) serve as a warning to us?

_____

_____

_____

3) What traditional (and highly meaningful) meals does your family celebrate?

_____

_____

_____

4) What does it mean to "glorify God" in our daily lives?

_____

_____

Background of the Passage

During the past several generations some of the strongest debate among fundamentalists and evangelicals has resolved around questionable practices—practices that many believers feel to be wrong but that are not specifically forbidden in Scripture. Some of the key issues have been drinking alcoholic beverages, smoking, card playing, wearing makeup, dancing, Sunday sports, styles of music, and going to the theater or movies. In later years the issues have ranged from visiting Disney Land to playing the lottery One reason Christians have spent so much time arguing those issues is that the Bible does not specifically forbid them. They are neither black nor white, but gray. Such issues in one age or area may not be the same as those in othe times or places; but every age and every place has had to deal with the gray areas of Christian living.

First Corinthians 8:1–11:1 features Paul's answers to questions posed by first-century believers struggling with their own gray area—the questionable practice in Corinth of eating food that had been offered to idols.

Here then is a masterful, highly practical passage on Christian liberty, what i means, and when we should voluntarily limit our freedom for the sake of "weaker" believers. In conclusion (10:23–30) Paul gives four principles for Christian liberty: (1) edification over gratification (v. 23); (2) others over self (v. 24); (3) liberty over legalism (vv. 25–27); and (4) condescension over condemnation (vv. 28–30).

Bible Passage

Read 1 Corinthians 8:1–11:1, noting the key words and definitions to the right of the passage.

1 Corinthians 8:1–11:1

¹ Now concerning things offered to idols: We know that we all have knowledge. Knowledge puffs up, but love edifies.

² And if anyone thinks that he knows anything, he knows nothing yet as he ought to know.

³ But if anyone loves God, this one is known by Him.

things offered to idols (v. 1)– The Greeks and Romans were polytheistic (worshiping many gods) and polydemonistic (believing in many evil spirits). They believed that evil spirits would try to invade human beings by attacking themselves to food before it was eaten, and that the spirits could be removed only by the food's being sacrificed to a god. The sacrifice was meant not only

⁴ *Therefore concerning the eating of things offered to idols, we know that an idol is nothing in the world, and that there is no other God but one.*

⁵ *For even if there are so-called gods, whether in heaven or on earth (as there are many gods and many lords),*

⁶ *yet for us there is one God, the Father, of whom are all things, and we for Him; and one Lord Jesus Christ, through whom are all things, and through whom we live.*

⁷ *However, there is not in everyone that knowledge; for some, with consciousness of the idol, until now eat it as a thing offered to an idol; and their conscience, being weak, is defiled.*

⁸ *But food does not commend us to God; for neither if we eat are we the better, nor if we do not eat are we the worse.*

⁹ *But beware lest somehow this liberty of yours become a stumbling block to those who are weak.*

¹⁰ *For if anyone sees you who have knowledge eating in an idol's temple, will not the conscience of him who is weak be emboldened to eat those things offered to idols?*

¹¹ *And because of your knowledge shall the weak brother perish, for whom Christ died?*

¹² *But when you thus sin against the brethren, and wound their weak conscience, you sin against Christ.*

¹³ *Therefore, if food makes my brother stumble, I will never again eat meat, lest I make my brother stumble.*

⁹:¹ *Am I not an apostle? Am I not free? Have I not seen Jesus Christ our Lord? Are you not my work in the Lord?*

² *If I am not an apostle to others, yet doubtless I am to you. For you are the seal of my apostleship in the Lord.*

³ *My defense to those who examine me is this:*

⁴ *Do we have no right to eat and drink?*

to gain favor with the god, but also to cleanse the meat from demonic contamination. Such decontaminated meat was offered to the gods as a sacrifice. That which was not burned on the altar was served at pagan feasts. What was left was sold in the market. After conversion, believers resented eating such food bought out of idol markets, because it reminded sensitive Gentile believers of their previous pagan lives and the demonic worship.

we all have knowledge (v. 1) —Paul and mature believers knew better than to be bothered by such food offered once to idols and then sold in the marketplace. They knew the deities didn't exist and that evil spirits did not contaminate the food.

love edifies (v. 1)—Knowledge mingled with love prevents a believer from exercising freedoms that offend weaker believers and, rather, builds the others up in truth and wisdom (see 13:1–4).

if anyone loves God (vv. 2–3) —Love is the proof of knowing God.

so-called gods (v. 5)—Some were outright fakes and some were manifestations of demons, but none were truly gods.

one God, the Father . . . one Lord Jesus Christ (v. 6)—A powerful and clear affirmation of the essential equality of God the Father and God the Son (see Eph. 4:4–6).

conscience . . . is defiled (v. 7)—The consciences of some newer converts did not allow them to eat idol food without feeling spiritually corrupted and guilty. They still imagined that idols were real and evil. A defiled conscience is one that has been violated, bringing fear, shame, and guilt.

commend us to God (v. 8)— The idea is of bringing us nearer to

⁵ *Do we have no right to take along a believing wife, as do also the other apostles, the brothers of the Lord, and Cephas?*

⁶ *Or is it only Barnabas and I who have no right to refrain from working?*

⁷ *Who ever goes to war at his own expense? Who plants a vineyard and does not eat of its fruit? Or who tends a flock and does not drink of the milk of the flock?*

⁸ *Do I say these things as a mere man? Or does not the law say the same also?*

⁹ *For it is written in the law of Moses, "You shall not muzzle an ox while it treads out the grain." Is it oxen God is concerned about?*

¹⁰ *Or does He say it altogether for our sakes? For our sakes, no doubt, this is written, that he who plows should plow in hope, and he who threshes in hope should be partaker of his hope.*

¹¹ *If we have sown spiritual things for you, is it a great thing if we reap your material things?*

¹² *If others are partakers of this right over you, are we not even more? Nevertheless we have not used this right, but endure all things lest we hinder the gospel of Christ.*

¹³ *Do you not know that those who minister the holy things eat of the things of the temple, and those who serve at the altar partake of the offerings of the altar?*

¹⁴ *Even so the Lord has commanded that those who preach the gospel should live from the gospel.*

¹⁵ *But I have used none of these things, nor have I written these things that it should be done so to me; for it would be better for me to die than that anyone should make my boasting void.*

¹⁶ *For if I preach the gospel, I have nothing to boast of, for necessity is laid upon me; yes, woe is me if I do not preach the gospel!*

¹⁷ *For if I do this willingly, I have a reward; but if against my will, I have been entrusted with a stewardship.*

God or making us approved by Him. Food is spiritually neutral.

stumbling block (vv. 9–11)—Some believers would be caused to fall back into old sins by getting involved with foods offered to idols.

perish (v. 11)—This is better translated "ruined," with the idea of "come to sin."

for whom Christ died (v. 11)—Christ died for all who believe, bearing the penalty for their sin and fully satisfying the wrath of God.

you sin against Christ (v. 12)—Paul warns that causing a brother or sister in Christ to stumble is more than simply an offense against that person; it is a serious offense against the Lord Himself.

seal of my apostleship (9:2)—The existence of the church in Corinth was evidence of Paul's apostolic authenticity.

examine (v. 3)—Using this Greek legal term for a preliminary investigation required before a decision was reached in a case, Paul sets out to defend his rights.

right to eat and drink (v. 4)—He was entitled to be married (v. 5) and to receive financial support from those to whom he ministered.

Cephas (v. 5)—Peter, who was married

working (v. 6)—With sarcasm, Paul, a tentmaker (Acts 18:3), let the Corinthians know that he and Barnabas had as much right as others to receive full financial support from their work. Except for help from a few churches, they paid their own expenses, not because of obligation or necessity, but voluntarily.

for our sakes (v. 10)—As in

18 What is my reward then? That when I preach the gospel, I may present the gospel of Christ without charge, that I may not abuse my authority in the gospel.

19 For though I am free from all men, I have made myself a servant to all, that I might win the more;

20 and to the Jews I became as a Jew, that I might win Jews; to those who are under the law, as under the law, that I might win those who are under the law;

21 to those who are without law, as without law (not being without law toward God, but under law toward Christ), that I might win those who are without law;

22 to the weak I became as weak, that I might win the weak. I have become all things to all men, that I might by all means save some.

23 Now this I do for the gospel's sake, that I may be partaker of it with you.

24 Do you not know that those who run in a race all run, but one receives the prize? Run in such a way that you may obtain it.

25 And everyone who competes for the prize is temperate in all things. Now they do it to obtain a perishable crown, but we for an imperishable crown.

26 Therefore I run thus: not with uncertainty. Thus I fight: not as one who beats the air.

27 But I discipline my body and bring it into subjection, lest, when I have preached to others, I myself should become disqualified.

10:1 Moreover, brethren, I do not want you to be unaware that all our fathers were under the cloud, all passed through the sea,

2 all were baptized into Moses in the cloud and in the sea,

3 all ate the same spiritual food,

4 and all drank the same spiritual drink. For they

agriculture, men should earn their living from their labor.

material things (v. 11)—financial support

others are partakers (v. 12)—Apparently, the church had financially supported other ministers.

endure (v. 12)—False teachers sought money. Paul wanted to be certain he was not classed with them, so he endured not accepting support, so as not to offend.

partake of the offerings (v. 13)—Old Testament priests were supported by the tithes of crops and animals, as well as by financial gifts.

live from the gospel (v. 14)—This refers to earning a living by preaching the good news.

none of these things (v. 15)—the six reasons given in verses 1–14 that indicate his right to financial support

nor have I written (v. 15)—He was not underhandedly hoping that, despite his protest, the Corinthians would feel obligated to pay him (2 Cor. 11:8–9).

better . . . to die (v. 15)—He preferred death to having anyone think he ministered with a financial motive.

make my boasting void (v. 15)—The term "boast" refers to that in which one glories or . . . the basis of one's glorying, and carries the idea of rejoicing. It is a statement of sincere joy, not pride (see 1:31). He was genuinely overjoyed at the privilege of serving the Lord and did not want material support to rob him of this joy in any way.

nothing to boast of (v. 16)—That is to say, his boast (see v. 15) was not personal. He was not proud as if it were his gospel; nor was he proud about the way he

drank of that spiritual Rock that followed them, and that Rock was Christ.

5 But with most of them God was not well pleased, for their bodies were scattered in the wilderness.

6 Now these things became our examples, to the intent that we should not lust after evil things as they also lusted.

7 And do not become idolaters as were some of them. As it is written, "The people sat down to eat and drink, and rose up to play."

8 Nor let us commit sexual immorality, as some of them did, and in one day twenty-three thousand fell;

9 nor let us tempt Christ, as some of them also tempted, and were destroyed by serpents;

10 nor complain, as some of them also complained, and were destroyed by the destroyer.

11 Now all these things happened to them as examples, and they were written for our admonition, upon whom the ends of the ages have come.

12 Therefore let him who thinks he stands take heed lest he fall.

13 No temptation has overtaken you except such as is common to man; but God is faithful, who will not allow you to be tempted beyond what you are able, but with the temptation will also make the way of escape, that you may be able to bear it.

14 Therefore, my beloved, flee from idolatry.

15 I speak as to wise men; judge for yourselves what I say.

16 The cup of blessing which we bless, is it not the communion of the blood of Christ? The bread which we break, is it not the communion of the body of Christ?

17 For we, though many, are one bread and one body; for we all partake of that one bread.

18 Observe Israel after the flesh: Are not those who eat of the sacrifices partakers of the altar?

19 What am I saying then? That an idol is anything, or what is offered to idols is anything?

necessity (v. 16)—Paul did not preach from personal pride, but from divine compulsion. He had no other choice, because God had sovereignly set him apart for service (see Jer. 1:5; 20:9; Acts 9:3–6, 15; Gal. 1:15; Col. 1:25).

woe (v. 16)—God's severest chastening is reserved for unfaithful ministers (Heb. 13:17).

against my will (v. 17)—This does not indicate that Paul was unwilling to obey, but that his will had no part in the call itself. Since it was God's sovereign choice and call, he received not a "reward" but a "stewardship" (a valuable responsibility or duty to be carefully managed).

my reward (v. 18)—Paul's reward was not money, but the privilege of preaching the gospel without support, so that he set aside his liberty ("right").

a servant (v. 19)—By choice, he set aside his right to be supported and "enslaved" himself to self-support in order to remove a potential offense and win more people to Jesus Christ (see Prov. 11:30).

became as a Jew (v. 20)—Within the limits of God's Word and his Christian conscience, Paul would be as culturally and socially Jewish as necessary when witnessing to Jews (see Rom. 9:3; 10:1; 11:14). He was not bound to the ceremonies and traditions of Judaism. All legal restraints had been removed, but there was the constraint of love (see Rom. 9:3; 10:1; 11:14).

those . . . without law (v. 21)—Gentiles; Paul was not suggesting the violating of God's moral law, but, as he explained, not being lawless toward God, but abiding by the law of Jesus Christ (see James 1:25)

20 Rather, that the things which the Gentiles sacrifice they sacrifice to demons and not to God, and I do not want you to have fellowship with demons.

21 You cannot drink the cup of the Lord and the cup of demons; you cannot partake of the Lord's table and of the table of demons.

22 Or do we provoke the Lord to jealousy? Are we stronger than He?

23 All things are lawful for me, but not all things are helpful; all things are lawful for me, but not all things edify.

24 Let no one seek his own, but each one the other's well-being.

25 Eat whatever is sold in the meat market, asking no questions for conscience' sake;

26 for "the earth is the LORD's, and all its fullness."

27 If any of those who do not believe invites you to dinner, and you desire to go, eat whatever is set before you, asking no question for conscience' sake.

28 But if anyone says to you, "This was offered to idols,"do not eat it for the sake of the one who told you, and for conscience' sake; for "the earth is the LORD's, and all its fullness."

29 "Conscience," I say, not your own, but that of the other. For why is my liberty judged by another man's conscience?

30 But if I partake with thanks, why am I evil spoken of for the food over which I give thanks?

31 Therefore, whether you eat or drink, or whatever you do, do all to the glory of God.

32 Give no offense, either to the Jews or to the Greeks or to the church of God,

33 just as I also please all men in all things, not seeking my own profit, but the profit of many, that they may be saved.

11:1 Imitate me, just as I also imitate Christ.

weak (v. 22)—He stooped to make the gospel clear at the lower level of comprehension, which Paul no doubt had done often while dealing with the Corinthians themselves (see 2:1–5).

all things . . . all means (v. 22) —Within the bounds of God's Word, he would not offend the Jew, Gentile, or those weak in understanding. Not changing Scripture or compromising the truth, he would condescend in ways that could lead to salvation.

race (v. 24)—The Greeks enjoyed two great athletic events, the Olympic games and the Isthmian games, and because the Isthmian events were held in Corinth, believers there were quite familiar with this analogy of running to win.

temperate (v. 25)—Self-control is crucial to victory.

crown (v. 25)—a wreath of greenery given to the winner of the race (see 2 Tim. 4:8)

not with uncertainty (v. 26)— Four times he has mentioned his goal of winning people to salvation (vv. 19–22).

beats the air (v. 26)—Paul changes the metaphor to boxing to illustrate the point that he was no shadow boxer, just waving his arms without effect.

discipline (v. 27)—from a term literally meaning to "hit under the eye"; Paul knocked out his bodily impulses to keep them from preventing him from fulfilling his mission of winning souls to Christ

disqualified (v. 27)—This is another metaphor from the athletic games. A contestant who failed to meet basic training requirements could not participate at all, much less have an opportunity to win. Paul may be especially referring to the fleshly sins that disqualify a man from preaching and leading the church, particularly emphasizing the need to be blameless and above reproach in the sexual area, since such sin is a disqualification.

Moreover . . . unaware (10:1)—This transition leads from the lack of self-discipline and subsequent disqualification spoken of in 9:27 to an illustration of it in ancient Israel.

all our fathers (v. 1)—Paul is referring to ancient Israel, of whom he was a descendant. In particular, he asked his readers to remember what had happened to Israel in the wilderness, because of freedom without self-control.

under the cloud (v. 1)—guided by God's presence as a cloud by day and column of fire at night (see Ex. 13:21)

through the sea (v. 1)—the Red Sea, which opened for Israel to pass through and closed to drown the Egyptian army (see Ex. 14:26–31)

baptized (v. 2)—Israel was immersed, not in the sea, but "into Moses," indicating their oneness, or solidarity, with him as their leader.

spiritual food . . . drink (vv. 3–4)—actual food provided by the spiritual power of God (see Ex. 17:6)

that spiritual Rock (v. 4)—The Jews had a legend that the actual rock Moses struck followed them throughout their wilderness wanderings, providing water for them. Paul says they have a Rock providing all they need, but it is Christ. Rock *(petra)* refers to a massive cliff, not simply a large stone or boulder, signifying the preincarnate Messiah (Christ), who protected and sustained His people.

not well pleased (v. 5)—This is an understatement. Because of Israel's extreme disobedience, God allowed only two of the men who had originally left Egypt (Joshua and Caleb) to enter the Promised Land; all the others died in the wilderness, including Moses and Aaron, who were disqualified from entering the Land (Num. 20:8–12, 24).

our examples (v. 6)—They died in the wilderness because of their failure of self-discipline and consequent indulgence of every desire (see note on 9:27). Four major sins characterized them: idolatry (v. 7); sexual immorality (v. 8); testing God (v. 9); and complaining (v. 10).

idolaters (v. 7)—The Israelites were barely out of Egypt when they fell into idol worship. Exodus 32 records the story (v. 6 is quoted here). Some three thousand were executed for instigating an immoral orgy at Sinai (Ex. 32:28).

play (v. 7)—a euphemism for the gross sexual relations that followed the excessive feasting

twenty-three thousand (v. 8)—Having just quoted from Exodus 32 in verse 7, this very likely also refers to the incident in Exodus 32, not to the incident at Shittim in Numbers 25 (contra marginal ref.). Apparently three thousand were killed by the Levites (Ex. 32:28) and twenty thousand died in the plague (Ex. 32:35).

tempt Christ (v. 9)—Numbers 21 records this story of the people questioning the goodness and plan of the One carrying them through the wilderness, the Protector and Provider, the spiritual Rock, Christ preincarnate (see note on v. 4).

destroyer (v. 10)—This incident is recorded in Num. 16:3–41. The same angel had slain the firstborn of the Egyptians (Ex. 12:23), the seventy thousand men because of David's census (2 Sam. 24:15–16), and the entire Assyrian army that was besieging Jerusalem (2 Chr. 32:21).

the ends of the ages (v. 11)—the time of Messiah; the last days of redemptive history before the messianic kingdom

who thinks he stands (v. 12)—The Bible is filled with examples of overconfidence (see Esth. 3–5; Is. 37:36–38; Rev. 3:1–3, 17).

temptation (v. 13)—See Matthew 6:13.

common to man (v. 13)—one Greek word, meaning "that which is human"

cup of blessing (v. 16)—The proper name given to the third cup during the Passover Feast. At the last Passover with the disciples, Jesus used the third cup as the symbol of His blood shed for sin. That cup became the one used to institute the Lord's Supper. He set the cup apart as a token of salvation blessing before passing it to the Twelve.

communion (v. 16)—This means "to have in common, to participate and have partnership with." The same Greek word is used in 1:9; Phil. 3:10. Commemorating the Lord's Supper was a regular and cherished practice in the early church, by which believers remembered their Savior's death and celebrated their common salvation and eternal life; sharing in Communion reflected their perfect spiritual oneness.

the blood of Christ (v. 16)—a vivid phrase used to represent Christ's sacrificial death and full atoning work; see Acts 20:28; Romans 3:25; Ephesians 1:7; Colossians 1:20; 1 Peter 1:19; 1 John 1:7; Revelation 1:5.

the bread (v. 16)—This symbolized our Lord's body as the cup symbolized His blood. Both point to His death as a sacrifice for the salvation of men.

are one bread (v. 17)—This refers to the bread of communion as the symbol of Christ's body given for all who believe. Since we all partake of that body, we are one. (see note on 6:17).

Observe Israel (v. 18)—In the Old Testament sacrifices, the offering was in behalf of all who ate (see Lev. 7:15–18). By such action, the people were identifying with the offering and affirming their devotion to God to whom it was offered. Paul was, by this, implying how any sacrifice made to an idol (see vv. 7, 14) was identifying with and participating with that idol. It is completely inconsistent for believers to participate in any such worship (v. 21).

jealousy (v. 22)—God tolerates no competition and will not allow idolatry to go unpunished (Deut. 32:21; Jer. 25:6, 9; see 11:30).

edify (v. 22)—to build up in Christian doctrine (see 8:1; 14:3–4, 26; Acts 20:32; 2 Cor. 12:19; Eph. 4:12; 2 Tim. 3:16–17)

the earth is the Lord's (v. 25)—Quoting Psalm 24:1, Paul declares that believers, though not participating in idol ceremonies (see notes on vv. 18–20), should not hesitate to buy and eat meat once used in such ceremonies.

eat whatever (v. 27)—so as not to offend the unbeliever

my liberty judged by another (v. 29)—Offending a weaker brother with one's freedom will cause the offended person to condemn us.

glory (v. 31)—Christian liberty, like all behavior, is to be conducted to the honor of God.

Understanding the Text

5) What was the specific situation in the Corinthian church that Paul addresses here?

_____

_____

_____

6) What counsel did Paul give the Corinthian believers regarding food sacrificed to idols (8:4–13)?

_____

_____

_____

(verses to consider: Mark 7:15; Acts 10:10–16; 1 Tim. 4:1–5)

7) When should a Christian voluntarily limit his or her liberty?

_____

_____

_____

8) Why was Paul so intent on living a disciplined life (9:27)?

_____

_____

_____

(verses to consider: Ps. 101:6; 1 Tim. 3:1–7; Titus 1:6–9)

9) Why did Paul write such strong words about idolatry to those who were believers?

_____

_____

_____

(verses to consider: Acts 17:29; Rom. 1:20–23; Gal. 5:19–21; Rev. 21:8; 22:14–15)

Cross Reference

Read Romans 14:1–23.

1 *Receive one who is weak in the faith, but not to disputes over doubtful things.*

2 *For one believes he may eat all things, but he who is weak eats only vegetables.*

3 *Let not him who eats despise him who does not eat, and let not him who does not eat judge him who eats; for God has received him.*

4 *Who are you to judge another's servant? To his own master he stands or falls. Indeed, he will be made to stand, for God is able to make him stand.*

5 *One person esteems one day above another; another esteems every day alike. Let each be fully convinced in his own mind.*

6 *He who observes the day, observes it to the Lord; and he who does not observe the day, to the Lord he does not observe it. He who eats, eats to the Lord, for he gives God thanks; and he who does not eat, to the Lord he does not eat, and gives God thanks.*

7 *For none of us lives to himself, and no one dies to himself.*

8 *For if we live, we live to the Lord; and if we die, we die to the Lord. Therefore, whether we live or die, we are the Lord's.*

9 *For to this end Christ died and rose and lived again, that He might be Lord of both the dead and the living.*

10 *But why do you judge your brother? Or why do you show contempt for your brother? For we shall all stand before the judgment seat of Christ.*

11 *For it is written:*
"As I live, says the LORD,
Every knee shall bow to Me,
And every tongue shall confess to God."

12 *So then each of us shall give account of himself to God.*

13 *Therefore let us not judge one another anymore, but rather resolve this, not to put a stumbling block or a cause to fall in our brother's way.*

14 *I know and am convinced by the Lord Jesus that there is nothing unclean of itself; but to him who considers anything to be unclean, to him it is unclean.*

15 *Yet if your brother is grieved because of your food, you are no longer walking in love. Do not destroy with your food the one for whom Christ died.*

16 *Therefore do not let your good be spoken of as evil;*

17 *for the kingdom of God is not eating and drinking, but righteousness and peace and joy in the Holy Spirit.*

18 *For he who serves Christ in these things is acceptable to God and approved by men.*

19 *Therefore let us pursue the things which make for peace and the things by which one may edify another.*

20 *Do not destroy the work of God for the sake of food. All things indeed are pure, but it is evil for the man who eats with offense.*

21 *It is good neither to eat meat nor drink wine nor do anything by which your brother stumbles or is offended or is made weak.*

22 *Do you have faith? Have it to yourself before God. Happy is he who does not condemn himself in what he approves.*

23 *But he who doubts is condemned if he eats, because he does not eat from faith; for whatever is not from faith is sin.*

Exploring the Meaning

10) How does this passage add to your understanding of how Christians should respond to the "gray areas" of life?

_____

_____

_____

11) Read 1 Timothy 5:17–18. When did Paul exercise his freedom as an apostle, and when did he voluntarily give up his rights?

_____

_____

_____

(verses to consider: Gal. 6:6; Acts 18:3; 20:34; 2 Thess. 3:8; 2 Cor.11:8–10)

12) Read Exodus 32:25–35. Why did Paul include a reference to this somber event in his letter to the Corinthians? What does this historical incident demonstrate about the holiness of God and the need for his people to strive for holiness? What does it say about overconfidence?

_____

_____

_____

(verses to consider: Prov. 16:18; Luke 22:33–34, 54–62; Mark 14:38; Heb. 12:3–4)

13) Read Isaiah 43:7. What does this verse say about why we were created and what our purpose on earth is? How should this affect our daily decisions and activities?

_____

_____

_____

(verses to consider: Ex. 9:16; 14:17–18; Ps. 29:1–2; Col. 1:16)

Summing Up . . .

"God is dishonored when anyone sins, but He is especially dishonored when His own people sin. Because He has specially honored us by His forgiving grace, we specially dishonor Him by our sin. When in justice He is forced to chastise us, He is further dishonored by unbelievers who charge, as did the nations around Israel and Judah, that He does not even take care of His own people. Sin of any sort takes glory from God.

"In the same way God is specially honored and glorified when His people are faithful and obedient. Just as our sin reflects against His honor, so our loving obedience reflects to His honor. When we resist and forsake sin we glorify our heavenly Father. And when we willingly use our Christian liberty for His sake and for the sake of His other children, we glorify Him still more."
—*John MacArthur*

Reflecting on the Text

14) Can you think of any actions or habits in your life that you might need to limit (so as not to offend a brother)?

_____

_____

_____

15) What promise or sobering example do you need to keep at the forefront of your mind as you battle temptation this week?

_____

_____

_____

16) What does the Lord's Supper mean to you? What are some specific ways you can make your next experience of communion more meaningful?

_____

_____

_____

17) List one or two practical ways you can remember to live out 1 Corinthians 10:31 today.

_____

_____

_____

Recording Your Thoughts

_____

_____

_____

For further study, see the following passages:

Genesis 14:18–21	Exodus 16:15	Numbers 18:8–24
Numbers 21:6	Deuteronomy 25:4	Psalm 115:4–7
Ezekiel 14:3; 36:23	Matthew 16:18; 18:6–14	Mark 1:29–31
Luke 1:13–17	Luke 22:17, 20	Acts 19:26; 26:13–19
Romans 15:17	2 Corinthians 8:1–5	Ephesians 2:13
Philippians 2:1; 3:17	Philippians 4:15–16	1 Thessalonians 2:9
1 Timothy 1:18	1 Timothy 4:3–5	2 Timothy 2:6
Hebrews 9:26	James 2:8, 12	James 3:1
1 Peter 1:4; 5:2	1 John 2:18; 4:19–5:1	1 John 5:21
Revelation 5:9	Revelation 21:8; 22:9	

Men & Women in the Church

1 Corinthians 11:2–16

Opening Thought

1) What are some of the areas in which your church would be viewed as "politically incorrect" by society?

_____

_____

_____

_____

_____

2) In what specific ways have you seen women's roles change since your childhood?

_____

_____

_____

_____

_____

3) How would you answer the charge that the church demeans women and relegates them to a second-class status?

_____

_____

_____

_____

Background of the Passage

The role of women has become a battleground in society during the last several decades. The struggle for women's rights has moved to an extreme feminism that threatens the future. In our day, the efforts of the enemy began with secular society and worked back into the church, which so often catches the world's diseases and adopts the spirit of the age. Some leaders and writers, in the name of Christianity, have gone so far as to teach principles that attempt to redefine, or even alter, biblical truths to accommodate the standards of contemporary thinking in the world. To do that, of course, they have to believe that Paul, Peter, and other scriptural writers added some of their own opinions to God's revealed truth or that the apostles sometimes taught culturally determined customs rather than divinely revealed standards. When that approach is taken, man must decide for himself what part of Scripture is revealed and what is not—making him the judge over God's Word. Satan feverishly tries to upset the divine order in any way he can, and one foundational way is by perverting male-female roles and relationships.

The Corinthian church faced similar problems and asked Paul for counsel on the subject of women's submission. Paul responded that there is no distinction between men and women as far as personal worth, intellect, or spirituality are concerned (see Gal. 3:28). That women function uniquely in God's order, however, submitting to their husband's authority, Paul affirms by several points: (1) the pattern in the Godhead (v. 3); (2) the divine design of male and female (v. 7); (3) the order of creation (v. 8); (4) the purpose of woman in regard to man (v. 9); (5) the concern of the angels (v. 10); and (6) the characteristics of natural physiology (vv. 13–15).

Bible Passage

Read 1 Corinthians 11:2–16, noting the key words and definitions to the right of the passage.

1 Corinthians 11:2–16

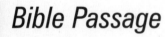

² *Now I praise you, brethren, that you remember me in all things and keep the traditions just as I delivered them to you.*

³ *But I want you to know that the head of every man is Christ, the head of woman is man, and the head of Christ is God.*

traditions (v. 2)—In the strict sense used here, a synonym for God's Word. The New Testament sometimes uses the word in a negative way, referring to man-made ideas or practices, especially those that conflict with Scripture.

⁴ *Every man praying or prophesying, having his head covered, dishonors his head.*

⁵ *But every woman who prays or prophesies with her head uncovered dishonors her head, for that is one and the same as if her head were shaved.*

⁶ *For if a woman is not covered, let her also be shorn. But if it is shameful for a woman to be shorn or shaved, let her be covered.*

⁷ *For a man indeed ought not to cover his head, since he is the image and glory of God; but woman is the glory of man.*

⁸ *For man is not from woman, but woman from man.*

⁹ *Nor was man created for the woman, but woman for the man.*

¹⁰ *For this reason the woman ought to have a symbol of authority on her head, because of the angels.*

¹¹ *Nevertheless, neither is man independent of woman, nor woman independent of man, in the Lord.*

¹² *For as woman came from man, even so man also comes through woman; but all things are from God.*

¹³ *Judge among yourselves. Is it proper for a woman to pray to God with her head uncovered?*

¹⁴ *Does not even nature itself teach you that if a man has long hair, it is a dishonor to him?*

¹⁵ *But if a woman has long hair, it is a glory to her; for her hair is given to her for a covering.*

¹⁶ *But if anyone seems to be contentious, we have no such custom, nor do the churches of God.*

Christ (v. 3)—Christ is the head of the church as its Savior and Lord (see Eph. 4:15). He is also the Lord over every unbeliever. Someday all will acknowledge His authority (see Phil. 2:10–11).

man (v. 3)—Men have authority over women in the basic order of creation (see vv. 8–9; see Is. 3:12; Eph. 5:22–33).

God (v. 3)—Christ has never been in any way inferior in essence to the Father, but in His incarnation He willingly submitted Himself to the Father's will in humble obedience.

covered, dishonors (v. 4)—Literally "having down from head," is probably a reference to men wearing a head covering, which seems to have been a local custom. Jews began wearing head coverings during the fourth century A.D., although some may already have been wearing them in New Testament times. Apparently, Corinthian men were doing the same, and Paul informs them that it is a disgrace. Paul is not stating a universal law from God, but acknowledging a local custom, which did reflect divine principle. In that society, a man's uncovered head was a sign of his authority over his wife, who was to have her head covered. For a man to cover his head was to suggest a reversal of proper roles.

woman who prays or prophesies (v. 5)—Paul makes clear directives that women are not to lead or speak in the services of the church, but they may pray and proclaim the truth to unbelievers, as well as teaching children and other women. Wherever and whenever women do pray and proclaim the Word appropriately, they must do so maintaining a proper distinction from men.

uncovered (v. 5)—In the culture of Corinth, a woman's covered head while ministering or worshiping was a symbol to signify a subordinate relationship to her husband. The apostle is not laying down an absolute law for women to wear veils or coverings in all churches for all time but is declaring that the symbols of the divinely established male and female roles are to be genuinely honored in every culture. As in the case of meat offered to idols (chaps. 8–9), there is nothing spiritual about wearing or not wearing a covering. But manifesting rebellion against God's order is wrong.

dishonors her head (v. 5)— "Head" may refer to her own self being disgraced by refusing to conform to recognized symbols of submission, or to her husband, who is disgraced by her behavior.

shameful . . . to be shorn (v. 6)—In that day only a prostitute or a feminist would shave her head. If a Christian woman rejected the covering that symbolized her submission in that culture, she might as well have shaved her head—the shame was similar.

image and glory of God (v. 7)—Though men and women were both created in God's image (Gen. 1:27), man's role uniquely reflects the glory of God. Like God, man is given a sphere of sovereignty as the earthly sovereign over God's created order.

woman is the glory of man (vv. 7–8)—As man carries authority delegated to him by God, so woman carries authority delegated to her by God through her husband. Man came from God; woman came from man (see Gen. 2:9–23; 1 Tim. 2:11–13).

angels (v. 10)—Women are to be submissive by wearing the symbol of authority so as not to offend these most holy and submissive creatures who watch the church (see Matt. 18:10; Eph. 3:9, 10), who were present at creation (Job 38:4, 7), when God designed the order of authority for men and women.

neither is man independent of woman, nor woman independent of man (vv. 11–12)—All believers, male and female, are equal in the Lord and complementary in the Lord's work. Their roles are different in function and relationships, not in spirituality or importance (see Gal. 3:28).

Is it proper (v. 13)—Aside from apostolic command, Paul asked, in effect, "Isn't it self-evident that women should not be uncovered?"

nature (vv. 14–15)—The term can convey the idea of basic human awareness, that is, the innate sense of what is normal and right. The male hormone, testosterone, speeds up the loss of hair in men. Estrogen causes women's hair to grow longer and for a longer time. Women are rarely bald, no matter how old. This physiology is reflected in most cultures in the custom of longer hair on women. God has given her hair as a covering to show tenderness, softness, and beauty.

no such custom (v. 16)—Neither the Lord, the apostles, nor the churches would allow female rebellion. Women were to maintain their distinctively feminine hairdos; and when custom dictated, they should wear a covering.

Understanding the Text

4) What specific worship practices was Paul addressing in this passage?

_____

_____

_____

5) How does Paul use the phrase "head of"—to imply superiority/inferiority or to suggest authority based on God's design? How do you know?

_____

_____

_____

_____

(verses to consider: Eph. 1:22–23; Col. 1:18; 1 Pet. 3:7)

6) How does Christ's willing submission to the Father serve as an example of how it is never demeaning to live out our God-appointed roles?

_____

_____

_____

_____

(verses to consider John 4:34; 5:30; 6:38; 1 Cor.3:23; 15:24–28; Phil. 2:3–11)

7) How do men represent the glory and image of God?

_____

_____

_____

_____

(verses to consider: Gen. 1:27; 2:7, 21–22)

Cross Reference

Read 1 Timothy 2:11–15.

¹¹ *Let a woman learn in silence with all submission.*
¹² *And I do not permit a woman to teach or to have authority over a man, but to be in silence.*

¹³ *For Adam was formed first, then Eve.*

¹⁴ *And Adam was not deceived, but the woman being deceived, fell into transgression.*

¹⁵ *Nevertheless she will be saved in childbearing if they continue in faith, love, and holiness, with self-control.*

Exploring the Meaning

8) What does this passage say about creation order and about the distinct roles of men and women?

_____

_____

_____

_____

_____

9) Read Titus 2:3–4. What teaching role does the New Testament allow women?

_____

_____

_____

_____

_____

10) Read Galatians 3:28. What does this passage say about the equality of men and women under God?

_____

_____

_____

_____

Summing Up . . .

"Lest men abuse their authority over women, Paul reminds them of their equality and mutual dependence. Man's authority was given by God to be used for His purposes and in His way. Man as a fellow creature has no innate superiority to women and has no right to use his authority tyrannically or selfishly. Male chauvinism is no more biblical than feminism. Both are perversions of God's plan.

"Far from oppressing women, the church has been their greatest liberator. In Greek and Roman societies most women were little more than slaves, the possessions of their husbands, who often virtually bought and traded their wives at will. It was largely because of this inhumane treatment of women that feminism became so popular in the Roman empire. In many Jewish communities the woman's situation was not much better. Divorce had become easy and commonplace, but it was almost entirely the prerogative of the man. Some Jewish men held women in such low esteem that they developed a popular prayer in which they thanked God that they were not born a slave, a Gentile, or a woman.

"But in Christ all believers, male and female, are in the Lord, and are alike under the Lord. In His work women are as important as men. Their roles are different in function and relationships, but not in spirituality or importance. . . . Men and women are complementary in every way in life, but particularly in the Lord's work do they function together as a divinely ordained team. They serve each other and they serve with each other. . . . Women are equal to men in the world, in the church, and before God. That is God's wise and gracious harmony and balance—difference in roles but equality in nature, personhood, work, and spirit. He created both for His glorious purposes."
—*John MacArthur*

Reflecting on the Text

11) What are some ways the truths in this passage could (and often are) misunderstood and/or distorted? How can you take what you've learned and clarify the erroneous assumptions of others this week?

_____

_____

_____

12) In what specific situations is it hardest for you to submit to a God-ordained authority? Why?

_____

_____

_____

_____

13) What part can you play in helping to promote healthy, biblical, God-honoring practices of worship in your own local church?

_____

_____

_____

_____

Recording Your Thoughts

_____

_____

_____

_____

_____

For further study, see the following passages:

Matthew 15:2–6	Matthew 28:18	John 10:30
John 17:21–24	Galatians 1:14	Colossians 2:8
2 Thessalonians 2:15	Hebrews 2:8	

The Lord's Supper

Opening Thought

1) Does your church ever sponsor potluck dinners, Wednesday night suppers, or Thanksgiving feasts, etc.? What are these occasions like?

_____

_____

_____

_____

2) Think back over your experience. What is the most meaningful celebration of the Lord's Supper you've ever been part of? What made that particular occasion so special?

_____

_____

_____

_____

3) If your pastor or church leaders asked you to plan the next communion service, what elements would you include so as to make it a profound time of worship for all?

_____

_____

_____

_____

Background of the Passage

By instruction and by example Christ instituted two ordinances, baptism and communion, ordinances that those who believe in Him are to follow faithfully. The present passage makes it clear that Paul had been obedient in establishing these ordinances in Corinth and that the believers there regularly celebrated the Lord's Supper.

The early church developed special fellowship meals that came to be called love feasts (Jude 12) and that usually closed with the observance of communion. These congregational meals stressed fellowship, affection, and mutual caring among the believers. The emphasis on oneness led very readily into a celebration of the unifying accomplishment of the Savior on the cross. The church at Corinth followed this custom, but, like those whom Peter condemns (2 Pet. 2:13), they had turned the meals into gluttonous, drunken revelry. Beyond that, wealthy believers brought ample food and drink for themselves but refused to share, letting their poorer brethren go away hungry (v. 21).Thus when the meal was connected to the bread and the cup remembrance, it was a flagrant desecration of the holy ordinance.

In calling the Corinthians to sanctity in their observance of the Lord's Supper, Paul discusses their perversion of it, the Lord's purpose for it, and the right preparation for it.

Bible Passage

Read 1 Corinthians 11:17–34, noting the key words and definitions to the right of the passage.

1 Corinthians 11:17–34

17 Now in giving these instructions I do not praise you, since you come together not for the better but for the worse.

18 For first of all, when you come together as a church, I hear that there are divisions among you, and in part I believe it.

19 For there must also be factions among you, that those who are approved may be recognized among you.

worse (v. 17)—a comparative Greek word that refers to moral evil

divisions (v. 18)—The church was torn by dissension.

approved . . . recognized (v. 19)—Factions revealed who passed the test of spiritual genuineness and purity.

20 Therefore when you come together in one place, it is not to eat the Lord's Supper.

21 For in eating, each one takes his own supper ahead of others; and one is hungry and another is drunk.

22 What! Do you not have houses to eat and drink in? Or do you despise the church of God and shame those who have nothing? What shall I say to you? Shall I praise you in this? I do not praise you.

23 For I received from the Lord that which I also delivered to you: that the Lord Jesus on the same night in which He was betrayed took bread;

24 and when He had given thanks, He broke it and said, "Take, eat; this is My body which is broken for you; do this in remembrance of Me."

25 In the same manner He also took the cup after supper, saying, "This cup is the new covenant in My blood. This do, as often as you drink it, in remembrance of Me."

26 For as often as you eat this bread and drink this cup, you proclaim the Lord's death till He comes.

27 Therefore whoever eats this bread or drinks this cup of the Lord in an unworthy manner will be guilty of the body and blood of the Lord.

28 But let a man examine himself, and so let him eat of the bread and drink of the cup.

29 For he who eats and drinks in an unworthy manner eats and drinks judgment to himself, not discerning the Lord's body.

30 For this reason many are weak and sick among you, and many sleep.

31 For if we would judge ourselves, we would not be judged.

32 But when we are judged, we are chastened by the Lord, that we may not be condemned with the world.

33 Therefore, my brethren, when you come together to eat, wait for one another.

34 But if anyone is hungry, let him eat at home, lest

---

it is not to eat the Lord's Supper (v. 20)—The love feast and Communion celebration had become so perverted that it was a sinful, selfish mockery. They could not legitimately say it was devoted to the Lord, since it was not honoring to Him.

Do you not have houses to eat and drink in? (vv. 21–22)—If they intended to selfishly indulge themselves, they might as well have stayed at home.

which I . . . delivered to you (vv. 23–26)—While the information was not new to the Corinthians, because Paul had previously "delivered" it, it is an important reminder. This description of Christ's final supper with his disciples is one of the most beautiful in all of Scripture, yet it was given in the midst of a strong rebuke of carnal selfishness. If this letter was written before any of the Gospels, as most conservative scholars believe, then Paul's instruction was the first biblical record of the institution of the Lord's Supper—given directly from the Lord and not through any other apostle or Evangelist (see Gal. 1:10–12).

broken (v. 24)—There is weak manuscript evidence for this word being included.

new covenant in My blood (v. 25)—The Old Covenant was practiced repeatedly by the blood of animals offered by men; but the New Covenant has been ratified once and for all by the death of Christ.

in remembrance of Me (v. 25) —Jesus transformed the third cup of the Passover into the cup of remembrance of His offering (see note on 10:16).

you proclaim (v. 26)—The gospel is presented through the

you come together for judgment. And the rest I will set in order when I come.

service of Communion as the elements are explained. They point to His physical incarnation, sacrificial death, resurrection, and coming kingdom.

in an unworthy manner (vv. 27, 29)—i.e., ritualistically, indifferently, with an unrepentant heart, a spirit of bitterness, or any other ungodly attitude

guilty (v. 27)—To come to the Lord's Table clinging to one's sin does not only dishonor the ceremony, but it also dishonors His body and blood, treating lightly the gracious sacrifice of Christ for us. It is necessary to set all sin before the Lord (v. 28), then partake, so as not to mock the sacrifice for sin by holding on to it.

judgment (v. 29)—i.e., chastisement

not discerning the Lord's body (v. 29)—When believers do not properly judge the holiness of the celebration of communion, they treat with indifference the Lord Himself—His life, suffering, and death.

sleep (v. 30)—In other words, they are dead. See note on 15:18. The offense was so serious that God put the worst offenders to death, an extreme but effective form of church purification.

we are chastened (v. 32)—Believers are kept from being consigned to hell, not only by divine decree, but by divine intervention. The Lord chastens to drive His people back to righteous behavior and even sends death to some in the church (v. 30) to remove them before they could be condemned.

Understanding the Text

4) In what way or ways were the Corinthians corrupting the celebration of the Lord's Supper?

_____

_____

_____

_____

5) What bedrock truths about the Lord's Supper does Paul teach in this passage? What is its purpose?

_____

_____

_____

_____

6) What sober instructions did Paul give the Corinthian Christians for preparing to participate in the Lord's Supper?

_____

_____

_____

_____

7) Paul speaks of communion as being a remembrance. What sort of things should Christians remember when partaking of the Lord's Supper?

_____

_____

_____

_____

(verses to consider: Matt. 26:26–29; Rom. 8:1; 2 Cor.5:17; Eph. 1:7; 1 Thess. 4:16–18)

Cross Reference

Read Exodus 12:1–14.

1 *Now the LORD spoke to Moses and Aaron in the land of Egypt, saying,*

2 *"This month shall be your beginning of months; it shall be the first month of the year to you.*

3 *"Speak to all the congregation of Israel, saying: 'On the tenth day of this month every man shall take for himself a lamb, according to the house of his father, a lamb for a household.*

4 *"And if the household is too small for the lamb, let him and his neighbor next to his house take it according to the number of the persons; according to each man's need you shall make your count for the lamb.*

5 *"Your lamb shall be without blemish, a male of the first year. You may take it from the sheep or from the goats.*

6 *"Now you shall keep it until the fourteenth day of the same month. Then the whole assembly of the congregation of Israel shall kill it at twilight.*

7 *"And they shall take some of the blood and put it on the two doorposts and on the lintel of the houses where they eat it.*

8 *"Then they shall eat the flesh on that night; roasted in fire, with unleavened bread and with bitter herbs they shall eat it.*

9 *"Do not eat it raw, nor boiled at all with water, but roasted in fire—its head with its legs and its entrails.*

10 *"You shall let none of it remain until morning, and what remains of it until morning you shall burn with fire.*

11 *"And thus you shall eat it: with a belt on your waist, your sandals on your feet, and your staff in your hand. So you shall eat it in haste. It is the LORD's Passover.*

12 *"For I will pass through the land of Egypt on that night, and will strike all the firstborn in the land of Egypt, both man and beast; and against all the gods of Egypt I will execute judgment: I am the LORD.*

13 *"Now the blood shall be a sign for you on the houses where you are. And when I see the blood, I will pass over you; and the plague shall not be on you to destroy you when I strike the land of Egypt.*

14 *"So this day shall be to you a memorial; and you shall keep it as a feast to the LORD throughout your generations. You shall keep it as a feast by an everlasting ordinance."*

Exploring the Meaning

8) How did Jesus transform the Jewish Passover celebration into a symbol of far greater significance?

_____

_____

_____

(verses to consider: Matt. 26:26–30; Mark 14:22–26; Luke 22:17–20)

9) Read Acts 2:42–47. How was the church at Corinth different from the church described here in Acts?

_____

_____

_____

10) Read Hebrews 9:28. How did the sacrifice of Christ that inaugurated the New Covenant (which is what Communion celebrates) differ from the sacrifices of the Old Covenant?

_____

_____

_____

Summing Up . . .

"Every time he comes to the Lord's Supper . . . a person should examine himself . . . . Before we partake we are to give ourselves a thorough self-examination, looking honestly at our hearts for anything that should not be there and sifting out all evil. Our motive, our attitudes toward the Lord and His Word, toward His people, and toward the Communion service itself should all come under private scrutiny before the Lord. The table thus becomes a special place for the purifying of the church. That is a vital use of Communion."—_John MacArthur_

Reflecting on the Text

11) How important is the Lord's Supper to you? How does this study change the way you view this ordinance?

_____

_____

_____

12) What instructions would you give a child before he or she took Communion for the first time?

_____

_____

_____

13) How do you intend to prepare yourself spiritually before you participate next time in the Lord's Supper?

_____

_____

_____

Recording Your Thoughts

_____

_____

_____

For further study, see the following passages:

Luke 13:1–5	John 13:2	John 19:33, 36
Acts 5:1–11	1 Corinthians 1:10–17	1 Corinthians 3:1–3
1 Thessalonians 2:4	1 John 5:16	Jude 24

Spiritual Gifts

Opening Thought

1) What are some of your unique gifts, attributes, and abilities? How do these serve a useful function at home, at work, in the church, and in other areas?

_____

_____

_____

2) If you had to give up one of your senses (sight, smell, taste, touch, or hearing), which would you choose to be without? How would it change your life to be without this "body part"?

_____

_____

_____

3) What person in your life personifies the notion of "love" and why?

_____

_____

_____

4) What practices and/or rituals in your church would seem really strange to an outsider?

_____

_____

_____

Background of the Passage

Perhaps no area of biblical doctrine has been more misunderstood and abused, even within evangelicalism, than that of spiritual gifts. Yet no area of doctrine is more important to the spiritual health and effectiveness of the church. Apart from the direct energizing of God's Spirit, nothing is more vital to believers than the ministry of their spiritual gifts, their God-given endowments for Christian service.

The Corinthian church, like much of the church today, was seriously affected by counterfeiting as well as by misunderstanding and misuse of spiritual gifts. Some of the Corinthian believers recognized the problem, and 1 Corinthians 12–14 continues to answer questions about which they had written Paul (7:1). Judging by the apostle's teaching in this section, the questions included: What are spiritual gifts? How many are there? Does every believer have them? How can a person know which one or ones he has? How important are they to individual Christian living and to the life of the church? What is the baptism of the Holy Spirit and how does it relate to spiritual gifts? Are all of the gifts given for every age of the church, or were some given only for a special purpose and a limited time? Can the gifts be counterfeited, and, if so, how can believers tell the true ones from the false? Those and many other questions Paul carefully answers.

In chapter 13 Paul writes about the root cause for the Corinthians' immature abuse of spiritual gifts—the failure to love. Throughout history it seems that the church has found it difficult to be loving. Thus, this sublime chapter—from a literary standpoint, arguably the greatest passage Paul ever penned—sets forth the proper attitude and atmosphere for the exercise of spiritual gifts in the church.

Bible Passage

Read 1 Corinthians 12:1–14:40, noting the key words and definitions to the right of the passage.

1 Corinthians 12:1–14:40

¹ Now concerning spiritual gifts, brethren, I do not want you to be ignorant:

² You know that you were Gentiles, carried away to these dumb idols, however you were led.

spiritual gifts (v. 1)—The NKJV translators italicized "gifts" to indicate that the word is not in the original but is implied by the context (see vv. 4, 9, 28, 30, 31; 14:1). The Greek literally means "pertaining to the Spirit," referring to that which

3 *Therefore I make known to you that no one speaking by the Spirit of God calls Jesus accursed, and no one can say that Jesus is Lord except by the Holy Spirit.*

4 *There are diversities of gifts, but the same Spirit.*

5 *There are differences of ministries, but the same Lord.*

6 *And there are diversities of activities, but it is the same God who works all in all.*

7 *But the manifestation of the Spirit is given to each one for the profit of all:*

8 *for to one is given the word of wisdom through the Spirit, to another the word of knowledge through the same Spirit,*

9 *to another faith by the same Spirit, to another gifts of healings by the same Spirit,*

10 *to another the working of miracles, to another prophecy, to another discerning of spirits, to another different kinds of tongues, to another the interpretation of tongues.*

11 *But one and the same Spirit works all these things, distributing to each one individually as He wills.*

12 *For as the body is one and has many members, but all the members of that one body, being many, are one body, so also is Christ.*

13 *For by one Spirit we were all baptized into one body—whether Jews or Greeks, whether slaves or free—and have all been made to drink into one Spirit.*

14 *For in fact the body is not one member but many.*

15 *If the foot should say, "Because I am not a hand, I am not of the body," is it therefore not of the body?*

16 *And if the ear should say, "Because I am not an eye, I am not of the body," is it therefore not of the body?*

17 *If the whole body were an eye, where would be the hearing? If the whole were hearing, where would be the smelling?*

has spiritual qualities or characteristics or is under some form of spiritual control. Spiritual gifts are divine enablements for ministry that the Holy Spirit gives in some measure to all believers and that are to be completely under His control and used for the building of the church to Christ's glory. These had to be distinguished from the mystical experiences called "ecstasy" (supernatural, sensuous communion with a deity) and "enthusiasm" (divination, dreams, revelations, visions) that were found in the pagan religions of Corinth.

Gentiles (v. 2)—that is, non-Christian pagans

carried away (v. 2)—Incredibly, some church members were mimicking certain dramatic and bizarre practices of the mystery religions in which they had been formerly involved. The practice of ecstasy, considered to be the highest expression of religious experience, involved supposed supernatural interaction with a deity, induced through frenzied hypnotic chants and ceremonies. The practice frequently included drunkenness (see Eph. 5:18) and sexual orgies, to which the devotees willfully yielded themselves to be led into gross sin.

accursed (v. 3)—This is the most severe kind of condemnation. Some of the Corinthians were fleshly and given over to ecstasies that were controlled by demons. In that condition, they actually claimed to be prophesying or teaching in the Spirit while demonically blaspheming the name of the Lord whom they were supposed to be worshiping. They had been judging the use of gifts on the basis of experience and not content. Satan always assaults the person of Christ. It is possible that the curser of Christ was a Gentile claiming to be a Christian but holding to a philosophy that all matter was evil, including the human Jesus (that is, pre-Gnosticism). He or she might have said that the Christ spirit left the human Jesus before His death, and therefore Jesus died a cursed death as a mere man.

¹⁸ *But now God has set the members, each one of them, in the body just as He pleased.*

¹⁹ *And if they were all one member, where would the body be?*

²⁰ *But now indeed there are many members, yet one body.*

²¹ *And the eye cannot say to the hand, "I have no need of you"; nor again the head to the feet, "I have no need of you."*

²² *No, much rather, those members of the body which seem to be weaker are necessary.*

²³ *And those members of the body which we think to be less honorable, on these we bestow greater honor; and our unpresentable parts have greater modesty,*

²⁴ *but our presentable parts have no need. But God composed the body, having given greater honor to that part which lacks it,*

²⁵ *that there should be no schism in the body, but that the members should have the same care for one another.*

²⁶ *And if one member suffers, all the members suffer with it; or if one member is honored, all the members rejoice with it.*

²⁷ *Now you are the body of Christ, and members individually.*

²⁸ *And God has appointed these in the church: first apostles, second prophets, third teachers, after that miracles, then gifts of healings, helps, administrations, varieties of tongues.*

²⁹ *Are all apostles? Are all prophets? Are all teachers? Are all workers of miracles?*

³⁰ *Do all have gifts of healings? Do all speak with tongues? Do all interpret?*

³¹ *But earnestly desire the best gifts. And yet I show you a more excellent way.*

^{13:1} *Though I speak with the tongues of men and of angels, but have not love, I have become sounding brass or a clanging cymbal.*

Jesus is Lord (v. 3)—Cf. Acts 2:36; Romans 10:9–10; Philippians 2:9–11. The validity of any speaking exercise is determined by the truthfulness of it. If the speaker affirms the lordship of Jesus, it is the truth from the Holy Spirit. What a person believes and says about Jesus Christ is the test of whether he speaks from the Holy Spirit, who always leads people to Christ's lordship (see 2:8–14; 1 John 5:6–8).

gifts (v. 4)—These categories of giftedness are not natural talents, skills, or abilities, such as are possessed by believers and unbelievers alike. They are sovereignly and supernaturally bestowed by the Holy Spirit on all believers (vv. 7, 11), enabling them to spiritually edify each other effectively and thus honor the Lord. The varieties of gifts fall into two general types: speaking and serving (see vv. 8–10). The speaking, or verbal, gifts (prophecy, knowledge, wisdom, teaching, and exhortation) and the serving, nonverbal gifts (leadership, helps, giving, mercy, faith, and discernment) are all permanent gifts that will operate throughout the church age. Their purpose is to edify the church and glorify God. The list here and in Romans 12:3–8 is best seen as representative of categories of giftedness which the Holy Spirit draws from to give each believer whatever kind or combination of kinds He chooses (v. 11). Some believers may be gifted categorically similar to others but they are all personally unique, as the Spirit suits each grace gift to the individual. Miracles, healing, languages, and the interpretation of languages were temporary sign gifts limited to the apostolic age and have, therefore, ceased. Their purpose was to authenticate the apostles and their message as the true Word of God, until God's written Word was completed and became self-authenticating. See notes on verses 9–10.

differences of ministries . . . diversities of activities
(vv. 5–6)—The Lord gives believers unique ministry arenas in which to

2 *And though I have the gift of prophecy, and understand all mysteries and all knowledge, and though I have all faith, so that I could remove mountains, but have not love, I am nothing.*

3 *And though I bestow all my goods to feed the poor, and though I give my body to be burned, but have not love, it profits me nothing.*

4 *Love suffers long and is kind; love does not envy; love does not parade itself, is not puffed up;*

5 *does not behave rudely, does not seek its own, is not provoked, thinks no evil;*

6 *does not rejoice in iniquity, but rejoices in the truth;*

7 *bears all things, believes all things, hopes all things, endures all things.*

8 *Love never fails. But whether there are prophecies, they will fail; whether there are tongues, they will cease; whether there is knowledge, it will vanish away.*

9 *For we know in part and we prophesy in part.*

10 *But when that which is perfect has come, then that which is in part will be done away.*

11 *When I was a child, I spoke as a child, I understood as a child, I thought as a child; but when I became a man, I put away childish things.*

12 *For now we see in a mirror, dimly, but then face to face. Now I know in part, but then I shall know just as I also am known.*

13 *And now abide faith, hope, love, these three; but the greatest of these is love.*

1 *Pursue love, and desire spiritual gifts, but especially that you may prophesy.*

2 *For he who speaks in a tongue does not speak to men but to God, for no one understands him; however, in the spirit he speaks mysteries.*

3 *But he who prophesies speaks edification and exhortation and comfort to men.*

4 *He who speaks in a tongue edifies himself, but he who prophesies edifies the church.*

fulfill their giftedness and provides varieties of power to energize and accomplish them (see Rom. 12:6).

manifestation of the Spirit (v. 7)—No matter what the gift, ministry, or effect, all spiritual gifts are from the Holy Spirit. They make Him known, understood, and evident in the church and in the world, by spiritually profiting all who receive their ministry.

the word of wisdom (v. 8)— "Word" indicates a speaking gift (see note on v. 4; see 1 Pet. 4:11). In the New Testament, "wisdom" is most often used of the ability to understand God's Word and His will, and to skillfully apply that understanding to life (see Matt. 11:19; Mark 6:2; Luke 7:35; Acts 6:10; James 1:5; 2 Pet. 3:15).

the word of knowledge (v. 8) —This gift may have been revelatory in the first century, but today it is the ability to understand and speak God's truth, with insight into the mysteries of His Word, that cannot be known apart from God's revelation (Rom. 16:25; Eph. 3:3; Col. 1:26; see 13:2). Knowledge majors on grasping the meaning of the truth; wisdom emphasizes the practical conviction and conduct that applies it.

faith (v. 9)—Distinct from saving faith or persevering faith, both of which all believers possess, this gift is exercised in persistent prayer and endurance in intercession, along with a strong trust in God in the midst of difficult circumstances (see Matt. 17:20).

healings (v. 9)—A temporary sign gift used by Christ (Matt. 8:16–17), the apostles (Matt. 10:1), the seventy (Luke 10:1), and a few associates of the apostles, such as Philip (Acts 8:5–7). This ability was identified as a gift belonging to the apostles (see 2 Cor. 12:12). Although Christians today do not have the gift of healings, God certainly still hears and answers the faithful prayers of His children. Some people feel that healing should be

⁵I wish you all spoke with tongues, but even more that you prophesied; for he who prophesies is greater than he who speaks with tongues, unless indeed he interprets, that the church may receive edification.

⁶ But now, brethren, if I come to you speaking with tongues, what shall I profit you unless I speak to you either by revelation, by knowledge, by prophesying, or by teaching?

⁷ Even things without life, whether flute or harp, when they make a sound, unless they make a distinction in the sounds, how will it be known what is piped or played?

⁸ For if the trumpet makes an uncertain sound, who will prepare himself for battle?

⁹ So likewise you, unless you utter by the tongue words easy to understand, how will it be known what is spoken? For you will be speaking into the air.

¹⁰ There are, it may be, so many kinds of languages in the world, and none of them is without significance.

¹¹ Therefore, if I do not know the meaning of the language, I shall be a foreigner to him who speaks, and he who speaks will be a foreigner to me.

¹² Even so you, since you are zealous for spiritual gifts, let it be for the edification of the church that you seek to excel.

¹³ Therefore let him who speaks in a tongue pray that he may interpret.

¹⁴ For if I pray in a tongue, my spirit prays, but my understanding is unfruitful.

¹⁵ What is the conclusion then? I will pray with the spirit, and I will also pray with the understanding. I will sing with the spirit, and I will also sing with the understanding.

¹⁶ Otherwise, if you bless with the spirit, how will he who occupies the place of the uninformed say "Amen" at your giving of thanks, since he does not understand what you say?

---

common and expected in every era, but this is not the case. Physical healings were very rare throughout the Old Testament period. Only a few are recorded. There was never a time before the coming of Christ when healings were common. Only in His lifetime and that of His apostles was there a veritable explosion of healing. This was due to the unique need to accredit the Messiah and to authenticate the first miracles of the gospel. To normalize healing would be to normalize the arrival of the Savior. This gift belonged to the sign gifts for that era only. The gift of healings was never used solely for bringing people physical health. Paul was sick but never healed himself or asked another human to heal him. His friend Epaphroditus was near death (Phil. 2:27), and Paul did not heal him. God intervened. When Timothy was sick Paul did not heal him but told him to take some wine (1 Tim. 5:23). Paul left Trophimus "sick at Miletus" (2 Tim. 4:20). Healings were not the everyday norm in Paul's ministry, but did occur when he entered a new region, e.g., Malta, where the gospel and its preacher needed authentication (see Acts 28:8, 9). That healing was the first mention of healing since the lame man was healed in Lystra (Acts 14:9) in connection with the arrival of Paul and the gospel there. Prior to that, the nearest healing was by Peter in Acts 9:34, and the resurrection of Tabitha in 9:41, so that people would believe the gospel Peter preached (9:42).

miracles (v. 10)—This temporary sign gift was for the working of divine acts contrary to nature, so that there was no explanation for the action except that it was by the power of God. This, too, was to authenticate Christ and the apostolic preachers of the gospel. John 2:11 notes that Jesus did His first miracle at Cana to "manifest His glory," not enhance the party (see John's purpose for recording the miracles of Jesus in this gospel, 20:30–31). Acts 2:22 affirms that Jesus did miracles to "attest" that God was working through Him, so that people would believe in Him as Lord and Savior. Jesus performed miracles

¹⁷ *For you indeed give thanks well, but the other is not edified.*

¹⁸ *I thank my God I speak with tongues more than you all;*

¹⁹ *yet in the church I would rather speak five words with my understanding, that I may teach others also, than ten thousand words in a tongue.*

²⁰ *Brethren, do not be children in understanding; however, in malice be babes, but in understanding be mature.*

²¹ *In the law it is written:*

*"With men of other tongues and other lips
I will speak to this people;
And yet, for all that, they will not hear Me,"
says the Lord.*

²² *Therefore tongues are for a sign, not to those who believe but to unbelievers; but prophesying is not for unbelievers but for those who believe.*

²³ *Therefore if the whole church comes together in one place, and all speak with tongues, and there come in those who are uninformed or unbelievers, will they not say that you are out of your mind?*

²⁴ *But if all prophesy, and an unbeliever or an uninformed person comes in, he is convinced by all, he is convicted by all.*

²⁵ *And thus the secrets of his heart are revealed; and so, falling down on his face, he will worship God and report that God is truly among you.*

²⁶ *How is it then, brethren? Whenever you come together, each of you has a psalm, has a teaching, has a tongue, has a revelation, has an interpretation. Let all things be done for edification.*

²⁷ *If anyone speaks in a tongue, let there be two or at the most three, each in turn, and let one interpret.*

²⁸ *But if there is no interpreter, let him keep silent in church, and let him speak to himself and to God.*

²⁹ *Let two or three prophets speak, and let the others judge.*

³⁰ *But if anything is revealed to another who sits by, let the first keep silent.*

and healed only for the three years of His ministry, not at all in the thirty years before. His miracles began when His ministry began. Though Jesus did miracles related to nature (made wine, created food, walked on water with Peter, ascended), no apostle ever is reported to have done a miracle in the natural realm. What miracles did the apostles do? The answer is in the word *miracles*, meaning "power," and is frequently connected to casting out demons (Luke 4:36; 6:18; 9:42). It is precisely that power that the Lord gave the disciples (Luke 9:1; 10:17–19; see also Acts 6:8; 8:7; 13:6–12).

prophecy (v. 10)—The meaning is simply that of "speaking forth," or "proclaiming publicly" to which the connotation of prediction was added sometime in the Middle Ages. Since the completion of Scripture, prophecy has not been a means of new revelation but is limited to proclaiming what has already been revealed in the written Word. Even the biblical prophets were preachers, proclaimers of God's truth both by revelation and reiteration. Old Testament prophets like Isaiah, Jeremiah, and Ezekiel spent lifetimes proclaiming God's Word. Only a comparatively small amount of what they preached is recorded in the Bible as God's direct revelation. They must have continually repeated and reemphasized those truths, as preachers today repeat, explain, and reemphasize the Word of God in Scripture. The best definition for this gift is given in 14:3. The importance of this gift is given in 14:1, 39. Its supremacy to other gifts, especially tongues, is the theme of chapter 14.

discerning of spirits (v. 10)— Satan is the great deceiver (John 8:44) and his demons counterfeit God's message and work. Christians with the gift of discernment have the God-given ability to recognize lying spirits and to identify deceptive and erroneous doctrine (see Acts 17:11; 1 John 4:1). Paul illustrated the use of this gift in Acts 16:16–18, as Peter had exercised it in Acts 5:3. When it was not being exercised in the Corinthian church, grave

³¹ *For you can all prophesy one by one, that all may learn and all may be encouraged.*

³² *And the spirits of the prophets are subject to the prophets.*

³³ *For God is not the author of confusion but of peace, as in all the churches of the saints.*

³⁴ *Let your women keep silent in the churches, for they are not permitted to speak; but they are to be submissive, as the law also says.*

³⁵ *And if they want to learn something, let them ask their own husbands at home; for it is shameful for women to speak in church.*

³⁶ *Or did the word of God come originally from you? Or was it you only that it reached?*

³⁷ *If anyone thinks himself to be a prophet or spiritual, let him acknowledge that the things which I write to you are the commandments of the Lord.*

³⁸ *But if anyone is ignorant, let him be ignorant.*

³⁹ *Therefore, brethren, desire earnestly to prophesy, and do not forbid to speak with tongues.*

⁴⁰ *Let all things be done decently and in order.*

distortion of the truth occurred (see v. 3; 14:29). Though its operation has changed since apostolic times (because of the completion of Scripture) it is still essential to have people in the church who are discerning. They are the guardians, the watchmen who protect the church from demonic lies, false doctrines, perverted cults, and fleshly elements. As it requires diligent study of the Word to exercise gifts of knowledge, wisdom, preaching, and teaching, so it does with discernment.

tongues . . . interpretation (v. 10)—These temporary sign gifts, using the normal words for speaking a foreign language and translating it, like the others (miracles, healings) were for the authentication of the truth and those who preached it. This true gift was clearly identified in Acts 2:5–12 as languages, which validated the gospel as divine. They were, however, because of their counterfeit in the culture, disproportionately exalted and seriously abused in Corinth. Here, Paul identified them, but throughout chapter 14 he discussed them in detail.

one and the same Spirit (v. 11)—While stressing the diversity of gifts (vv. 4–11), Paul also stressed the singular source in the Spirit (see vv. 4–6, 8–9.) This is the fifth mention, in this chapter, of the source of gifts being the Holy Spirit. It emphasizes that gifts are not something to seek, but to be received from the Spirit "as He wills." It is He alone who "works" or energizes (v. 6) all gifts as He chooses.

body . . . members (v. 12)— Paul used the human body as an analogy (see 10:17) for the unity of the church in Christ. From this point on to verse 27, he used "body" eighteen times (see Rom. 12:5; Eph. 1:23; 4:4, 12, 16; Col. 1:18).

baptized (v. 13)—The church, the spiritual body of Christ, is formed as believers are immersed by Christ with the Holy Spirit. Christ is the baptizer who immerses each believer with the Spirit into unity with all other believers. Paul is not writing of water baptism. That outward sign depicts the believer's union with Christ in His death and resurrection (see Rom. 6:3–5). Similarly, all believers are also immersed into the body of Christ by means of the Holy Spirit. Paul's point is to emphasize the unity of believers. There cannot be any believer who has not been Spirit-baptized, nor can there be more than one Spirit baptism or the whole point of unity in the body of Christ is distorted. Believers have all been Spirit-baptized and thus are all in one body. This is not an experience to seek, but a reality to acknowledge. (see Acts 11:15–17).

drink into one Spirit (v. 13)—At salvation, all believers not only become full members of Christ's body, the church, but the Holy Spirit is placed within each of them (Rom. 8:9; see 6:19; Col. 2:10; 2 Pet. 1:3–4). There is no need (or divine provision) for any such thing as a second blessing, a triumphalistic experience of a deeper life, or a formula for instantly increased spirituality (see John 3:34). Christ's salvation provision is perfect and He calls only for obedience and trust in what has already been given (Heb. 10:14).

no need (v. 21)—While some in Corinth were bemoaning the fact that they did not have the showy gifts (see note on vv. 14–20), those who did were belittling those with the more quiet and less prominent gifts. The "eye" and the "head," which are highly visible and the focus of all who engage each other, represent the people with public gifts. They so overestimated their own importance that they disdained those whom they perceived as less gifted and less significant. They were apparently indifferent ("I have no need") and self-sufficient.

God has appointed (vv. 28–30)—Again emphasizing the sovereignty of God (see vv. 7, 11, 18), Paul illustrates the individuality and unity of the body by a repetition of the representative categories of ministries, callings, and giftedness.

apostles . . . prophets (v. 28)—Their purpose was (1) to lay the foundation of the church (Eph. 2:20); (2) to receive and declare the revelation of God's Word (Acts 11:28; 21:10–11; Eph. 3:5); and (3) to give confirmation of that Word through signs, wonders, and miracles (2 Cor. 12:12; see Acts 8:6–7; Heb. 2:3–4). "Apostles" refers, primarily, to those twelve chosen by our Lord plus Paul and Matthias (Acts 1:26). In a secondary sense, others served as messengers of the church: Barnabas (Acts 14:14), Silas and Timothy (1 Thess. 2:6), and others (Rom. 16:7; 2 Cor. 8:23; Phil. 2:25). Apostles of Christ were the source of the church's doctrine (Acts 2:42); apostles of the church (2 Cor. 8:23) were its early leaders. "Prophets" were especially gifted men in the local churches, who preached God's Word (Acts 11:21–28; 13:1). Any message preached by a prophet had to be judged by the word of the apostles (see note on 14:36–37).

teachers (v. 28)—Could be the same as pastor-teachers (see Eph. 4:11), but probably should be broadened to include all who are gifted for teaching in the church, whether they have the office of pastor or not.

miracles . . . healings . . . tongues (v. 28)—See notes on verses 9–10.

helps, administration (v. 28)—These less public gifts are mingled with the more public manifestations of the Spirit to show their vital necessity (v. 22). "Helps" is an ability for service; in fact, the gift of ministry ("service") in Rom. 12:7 is in the same category. "Administration" is leadership. The word comes from the Greek, meaning "to pilot a ship" (Acts 27:11) and speaks of one who can lead ministries of the church efficiently and effectively.

earnestly desire (v. 31)—In context, this could not mean that believers should desire the more prominent gifts, when the whole chapter has just been confronting the fact that they have sinfully been doing just that. Desiring gifts for selfish reasons is wrong, since they are sovereignly given by God as He wills (vv. 7, 11, 18, 28). Therefore, this must be rendered not as an imperative (command), but, as the verb form allows, as an indicative (statement of fact), "You are desiring the showy gifts, wrongly." The real imperative is to stop doing that and learn the "more excellent way," the way of love, which Paul will explain in chapter 13.

tongues of men (13:1)—That this gift was actual languages is established in Acts 2:4–12, affirmed in this text by Paul's calling it "of men"—clearly a reference to human language. This was the gift which the Corinthians prized so highly, abused so greatly, and counterfeited so disastrously. God gave the ability to speak in a language not known to the speaker as a sign with limited function (see notes on 14:1–33).

tongues . . . of angels (v. 1)—The apostle was writing in general, hypothetical terms. There is no biblical teaching of any special angelic language that people could learn to speak.

love (v. 1)—Self-giving love is more concerned with giving than receiving (John 3:16; see 14:1; Matt. 5:44–45; John 13:1; 15:9; Rom. 5:10; Eph. 2:4–7; Phil. 2:2; Col. 3:14; Heb. 10:24). The word used here, *agape*, was seldom used in ancient Greek literature, but it is common in the New Testament. Without love, no matter how gifted one is to speak his own language, other languages, or even (hypothetically) the speech of angels, his speech is noise only. In New Testament times, rites honoring the pagan deities Cybele and Bacchus (or Dionysus) included ecstatic noises accompanied by gongs, cymbals, and trumpets. Unless the speech of the Corinthians was done in love, it was no better than the gibberish of pagan ritual.

the gift of prophecy (v. 2)—See notes on 12:10. In 14:1–5, Paul speaks of this gift as the most essential one because it brings God's truth to people. Even this gift must be ministered in love (see Eph. 4:15).

understand all mysteries and all knowledge (v. 2)—This encompasses gifts of wisdom, knowledge, and discernment (see notes on 12:8, 10), which are to be exercised in love.

all faith (v. 2)—This refers to the gift of faith (enduring, believing prayer; see note on 12:9), which is useless without selfless love for the church.

burned (v. 3)—The practice of burning Christians at the stake did not begin until some years later, but it was clearly understood to be an extremely horrible death. Neither volunteering for giving up all your possessions or being burned would produce any spiritual benefit if not done out of love for the body of Christ.

never fails (vv. 8–10)—This refers to love's lastingness or permanence as a divine quality. Love outlasts all failures (see 1 Pet. 4:8). Paul strengthens his point on the permanence of love by comparing it to the spiritual gifts which the Corinthians so highly prized: prophecy, knowledge, and languages, all of which will have an end. There may be a distinction made on how prophecy and knowledge come to an end, and how the gift of languages does. This is indicated by the Greek verb forms used. In the case of prophecy and knowledge, they are both said to "be abolished" (in both cases the verb indicates that something will put an end to those two functions). Verses 9–10 indicate that what will abolish knowledge and prophecy is "that which is perfect." When that occurs, those gifts will be rendered inoperative. The "perfect" is not the completion of Scripture, since there is still the operation of those two gifts and will be in the future kingdom (see Joel 2:28; Acts 2:17; Rev. 11:3). The Scriptures do not allow us to see "face to face" or have perfect knowledge as God does (v. 12). The "perfect" is not the rapture of the church or the second coming of Christ, since the kingdom to follow these events will have an abundance of preachers and teachers (see Is. 29:18; 32:3–4; Joel 2:28; Rev. 11:3). The perfect must be the eternal state, when we in glory see God face to face (Rev. 22:4) and have full knowledge in the eternal new heavens and new earth. Just as a child grows to full understanding, believers will come to perfect knowledge and no such gifts will be necessary. On the other hand, Paul uses a different word for the end of the gift of languages, thus indicating it will "cease" by itself, as it did at the end of the apostolic age. It will not end by the coming of the "perfect," for it will already have ceased. The uniqueness of the gift of languages and its interpretations was, as all sign gifts, to authenticate the message of the gospel before the New Testament was completed (Heb. 2:3–4). "Tongues" was also limited by being a judicial sign from God of Israel's judgment (see note on 14:21; see Is. 28:11–12). "Tongues" was also not a sign to believers, but unbelievers (see note on 14:22), specifically those unbelieving Jews. Tongues also ceased because there was no need to verify the true messages from God once the Scripture was given. It became the standard by which all are to be deemed true. "Tongues" was a means of edification in a way far inferior to preaching and teaching (see notes on 14:5, 12–13, 27–28). In fact, chapter 14 was designed to show the Corinthians, so preoccupied with tongues, that it was an inferior means of communication (vv. 1–12), an inferior means of praise (vv. 13–19), and an inferior means of evangelism (vv. 20–25). Prophecy was, and is, far superior (vv. 1, 3–6, 24, 29, 31, 39). That tongues ceased should be clear from its absence from all other books in the New Testament, except Acts. Tongues ceased to be an issue of record or practice in the early church, as the Scripture was being written. That tongues have ceased also should be clear from their absence through church history since the first century, appearing only sporadically and then only in questionable groups. A more detailed discussion is given in the notes on chapter14.

love (v. 13)—The objects of faith and hope will be fulfilled and perfectly realized in heaven, but love, the Godlike virtue, is everlasting (see 1 John 4:8). Heaven will be the place for the expression of nothing but perfect love toward God and each other.

Pursue love (14:1)—This is a command for every believer. Because lovelessness was a root spiritual problem in the Corinthian church, the godly love just described should have been sought after by them with particular determination and diligence.

desire spiritual gifts (v. 1)—Love does not preclude the use of these enablements. Since Paul has addressed not desiring showy gifts (12:31) and not elevating one over the other (12:14–25), some might think it best to set them all aside for unity's sake. Spiritual gifts, on the other hand, are sovereignly bestowed by God on each believer and necessary for the building of the church (12:1–10). Desire for them, in this context, is in reference to their use collectively and faithfully in His service—not a personal yearning to have an admired gift that one did not possess. As a congregation, the Corinthians should be wanting the full expression of all the gifts to be exercised. The command is in the plural emphasizing the corporate desire of the church.

especially . . . prophesy (v. 1)—This spiritual gift was desirable in the life of the church to serve in a way that tongues cannot, namely, by edifying the entire church (v. 5).

he who speaks in a tongue (v. 2)—This is singular (see previous note; see vv. 4, 13–14, 19, 27), indicating that it refers to the false gibberish of the counterfeit pagan ecstatic speech. The singular is used because gibberish can't be plural; there are not various kinds of non-language. There are, however, various languages; hence when speaking of the true gift of language, Paul uses the plural to make the distinction (vv. 6, 18, 22–23, 29). The only exception is in vv. 27–28 (see note there), where it refers to a single person speaking a single genuine language.

no one understands him; . . . in the spirit he speaks mysteries (v. 2)—The carnal Corinthians using the counterfeit ecstatic speech of paganism were not interested in being understood, but in making a dramatic display. The spirit by which they spoke was not the Holy Spirit, but their own human spirit or some demon; and the mysteries they declared were the type associated with the pagan mystery religions, which only the initiated few were said to know and understand. Those mysteries were totally unlike the ones mentioned in Scripture, which are divine revelations of truths previously hidden (see notes on 12:7).

does not speak to men but to God (v. 2)—This is better translated "to a god." The Greek text has no definite article (see similar translation in Acts 17:23, "an unknown god"). Their gibberish was worship of pagan deities. The Bible records no incident of any believer ever speaking to God in any other than normal human language.

prophesies (v. 3)—In dramatic contrast to the bedlam of counterfeit tongues was the gift of genuine prophesy or preaching of the truth (see note on 12:10). It produced the building up in truth, the encouragement to obedience, and the comfort in trouble that God desired for His church. Spiritual gifts are always for the benefit of others, never oneself.

a tongue (v. 4)—Again (as in v. 2), Paul uses the singular to refer to the pagan counterfeit gibberish and sarcastically marks its selfishness as some kind of self-edification (see v. 16; 4:8–10 for other sarcasm). This illicit building up of self comes from pride-induced emotion, which only produces more pride.

all spoke with tongues . . . that you prophesied (v. 5)—Here the plural, "tongues," appears as Paul was referring to the real gift of languages (see note on v. 2). Obviously this was not Paul's true desire, even for the true gift, since the very idea was impossible and contrary to God's sovereign distribution of gifts (12:11, 30). He was simply suggesting hypothetically that, if they insisted on clamoring after gifts they did not possess, they at least should seek the one that was more enduring and more valuable for the church. The only purpose tongues renders to the church is when it is interpreted (the normal Greek word for translation). Wherever God gave the gift of languages, He also gave the gift for translation, so that the sign would also be edifying. Never was the gift to be used without such translation (v. 28), so that the church would always be edified.

if I come to you . . . what shall I profit? (v. 6)—Even an apostle who spoke in tongues did not spiritually benefit a congregation unless, through interpretation, his utterance was clarified so that the revelation and knowledge could be understandably preached and taught. Any private use of this gift is excluded for several reasons: (1) it is a sign to unbelievers (v. 22); (2) it must have a translator to have any meaning, even to the speaker (v. 2); and (3) it must edify the church (v. 6).

uninformed (v. 16)—from the Greek word meaning "ignorant" or "unlearned"

I speak with tongues more than you all (v. 18)—Paul emphasized that by writing all of this, he was not condemning genuine tongues (plural); nor, as some may have thought to accuse him, was he envious of a gift he did not possess. At that point, he stopped speaking hypothetically about counterfeit tongue-speaking. He actually had more occasions to use the true gift than all of them (though we have no record of a specific instance). He knew the true gift and had used it properly. It is interesting, however, that the New Testament makes no mention of Paul's actually exercising that gift. Nor does Paul in his own writings make mention of a specific use of it by any Christian.

teach others (v. 19)—This is the general principle that summarizes what he has been saying, that is, teaching others is the important matter and that requires understanding.

in malice be babes, but in understanding be mature (v. 20)—Most of the Corinthian believers were the opposite of what Paul here admonished. They were extremely experienced in evil, but greatly lacking in wisdom. Yet mature understanding was especially essential for proper comprehension and use of the gift of tongues, because the conspicuous and fascinating nature of that gift made it so attractive to the flesh. He was asking his readers to put aside emotion and experience, along with the desires of the flesh and pride, to think carefully about the purpose of tongues.

it is written (v. 21)—In a freely rendered quotation from Is. 28:11–12, Paul explains that centuries earlier the Lord had predicted that one day He would use men of other tongues, that is, foreigners speaking unknown languages, as a sign to unbelieving Israel, who "will not hear Me." These "other tongues" are what they knew as the gift of languages, given solely as a sign to unbelieving Israel. That sign was threefold: cursing, blessing, and authority. To emphasize the cursing, Paul quoted Isaiah's words of warning to Judah of the judgment from Assyria. The leaders thought his words were too simple and rejected him. The time would come, the prophet said, when they would hear Assyrian, a language they could not understand, indicating judgment. Jeremiah spoke similarly of the Babylonians who were also to come and destroy Judah (see Jer. 5:15). When the apostles spoke at Pentecost in various foreign languages (Acts 2:3–12), the Jews should have known that the judgment prophesied and historically fulfilled first by the Assyrians and then by the Babylonian captivity was about to fall on them again for their rejection of Christ, including the destruction of Jerusalem (A.D. 70) as had happened in 586 B.C. under Babylonian power.

Therefore tongues are for a sign, not to those who believe but to unbelievers (v. 22)— Explaining further, he says explicitly that all tongues are for the sake of unbelievers. In other words, that gift has no purpose in the church when everyone present is a believer. And once the sign served its purpose to pronounce judgment or cursing on Israel, and the judgment fell, the purpose ceased along with the sign gift. The blessing of that sign was that God would build a new nation of Jews and Gentiles to be his people (Gal. 3:28), to make Israel jealous and someday repent (see Rom. 11:11–12, 25–27). The sign was thus repeated when Gentiles were included in the church (Acts 10:44–46). The sign also gave authority to those who preached both the judgment and blessing (2 Cor. 12:12), including Paul (v. 18).

but prophesying is . . . for those who believe (v. 22)—In the completely opposite way, the gift of prophesying benefits only believers, who are able, by their new natures and the indwelling Holy Spirit, to understand spiritual truth (see 2:14; 1 John 2:20, 27).

Therefore if . . . all speak with tongues (v. 23)—As Paul explains in more detail later (vv. 27–28), even for unbelievers, even when the gift of tongues was exercised in its proper time in history, when it was dominant and uncontrolled in the church, bedlam ensued and the gospel was disgraced and discredited.

out of your mind (v. 23)—The Greek word means to be in an uncontrolled frenzy. When the real gift was used in Acts 2, there was no madness, and everyone understood in his own language (v. 11). In Corinth, there was charismatic chaos.

But if all prophesy (vv. 24–25)—This means to publicly proclaim the Word of God (see note on 2:10). "All" does not mean all at once (see v. 31), but rather means that hypothetically if the cacophony of all the Corinthians could be replaced by all of them preaching the Word, the effect on unbelievers would be amazingly powerful, the gospel would be honored, and souls would be converted to worshiping God.

each of you has (v. 26)—It seems that chaos and lack of order was rampant in that assembly (v. 33). It is interesting that no elders or pastors are mentioned, and the prophets were not even exercising control (see vv. 29, 32, 37). Everyone was participating, with whatever expression they desired, whenever they desired.

a psalm (v. 26)—the reading or singing of an Old Testament psalm

a teaching (v. 26)—This probably refers to a doctrine or subject of special interest (v. 33).

a tongue (v. 26)—In the singular, this refers to the counterfeit.

a revelation (v. 26)—some supposed word from God, whether spurious or genuine

an interpretation (v. 26)—This refers to that of a tongue's message.

for edification (v. 26)—This was Paul's way of calling a halt to the chaos. Edification is the goal (see vv. 3–5, 12, 17, 26, 31), and the Corinthian chaos could not realize it.

confusion (v. 33)—Here is the key to the whole chapter. The church at worship before God should reflect His character and nature because He is a God of peace and harmony, order and clarity, not strife and confusion (see Rom. 15:33; 2 Thess. 3:16; Heb. 13:20).

as in all the churches (v. 33)—This phrase does not belong in verse 33, but at the beginning of verse 34, as a logical introduction to a universal principle for churches.

women keep silent in the churches (vv. 34–35)—The principle of women not speaking in church services is universal; this applies to all the churches, not just locally, geographically, or culturally. The context in this verse concerns prophecy, but includes the general theme of the chapter, that is, tongues. Rather than leading, women are to be submissive, as God's Word makes clear (see notes on 11:3–15). It is not coincidental that many modern churches that have tongues-speaking and claim gifts of healings and miracles also permit women to lead worship, preach, and teach. Women may be gifted teachers, but they are not permitted by God "to speak" in churches. In fact, for them to do so is "shameful," meaning "disgraceful." Apparently, certain women were out of order in disruptively asking questions publicly in the chaotic services.

did the word of God come . . . from you? (v. 36)—See 1 Thess. 2:13.

ignorant (v. 38)—That is, anyone who does not recognize the authority of Paul's teaching should himself not be recognized as a legitimate servant gifted by God.

do not forbid . . . tongues (v. 39)—Legitimate languages were limited in purpose and in duration, but as long as this gift was still active in the early church, it was not to be hindered. But prophecy was the most desirable gift to be exercised because of its ability to edify, exhort, and comfort with the truth (v. 3).

Understanding the Text

5) What is the source and purpose of spiritual gifts?

_____

_____

(verses to consider: Mark 10:45; Eph. 4:11–16)

6) How does Paul's analogy of the body demonstrate both the unity and diversity of the church?

_____

_____

7) What does Paul say here to demonstrate that God designed the members of the body of Christ to be interdependent, rather than independent?

_____

_____

(verses to consider: John 13:34; Rom. 12:10, 16; 13:8; Gal. 5:13; Eph. 4:1–3; 5:19–21; Col. 3:12–16)

8) How did Paul describe the love that should mark God's people?

_____

_____

9) What instructions did Paul give to insure that worship was carried out in an orderly way?

_____

_____

Cross Reference

Read Romans 12:4-8.

⁴ *For as we have many members in one body, but all the members do not have the same function,*

⁵ *so we, being many, are one body in Christ, and individually members of one another.*

⁶ *Having then gifts differing according to the grace that is given to us, let us use them: if prophecy, let us prophesy in proportion to our faith;*

⁷ *or ministry, let us use it in our ministering; he who teaches, in teaching;*

⁸ *he who exhorts, in exhortation; he who gives, with liberality; he who leads, with diligence; he who shows mercy, with cheerfulness.*

Exploring the Meaning

10) What does this passage say about spiritual gifts? Do you think this list,

together with the list in 1 Corinthians 12, represent *all* the gifts available to believers? Why or why not?

_____

_____

11) Read 1 Peter 4:10–11. How does this passage shatter any notion that spiritual gifts should be a source of sinful pride?

_____

_____

12) Read Isaiah 28:9–12. In what way were tongues intended as a sign of judgment on the Jews as well as a sign of blessing to the Gentiles?

_____

_____

(verses to consider: Deut. 28:49; Jer. 5:15; Acts 10:44–46)

Summing Up . . .

"The Bible's simplest description of God—and therefore God's own description of Himself—is 'God is love' (1 John 4:16). Love is the most blessed manifestation of the character of God. John continues, 'and the one who abides in love abides in God, and God abides in him' (v. 16b). Therefore the simplest and most profound description of Christian character also is love.

"It is tragic that in many churches, as in the one in ancient Corinth, the love that is basic to Christian character does not characterize the membership or the ministry."—*John MacArthur*

Reflecting on the Text

13) In what precise ways can you show and share God's infinite, matchless love with someone else today?

_____

_____

_____

14) Based on what you've studied (as well as on your prior experiences of service), what spiritual gift(s) do you think you have been given? How can you use your gift(s) this week to build up others in your church?

_____

_____

_____

15) Make a list of three people whom you will contact in the coming week for the purpose of expressing appreciation to them for their faithfulness in using their spiritual gift to encourage you.

_____

_____

_____

Recording Your Thoughts

_____

_____

_____

For further study, see the following passages:

Genesis 3:16	Matthew 13:11; 13:54	John 13:34–35
John 15:26	Acts 8:17	Acts 10:44–45
Acts 17:11	Acts 19:14–16	Romans 15:2–3
Ephesians 1:20–21	Ephesians 2:16	Ephesians 3:3–9
Ephesians 4:4–6	Philippians 1:9	Colossians 2:2 1
Thessalonians 4:5	1 Thessalonians 5:11	1 Thessalonians 5:20–22
1 Timothy 2:11–15	2 Timothy 3:15–17	James 3:13, 17
James 5:13–16	1 Peter 2:12	2 Peter 1:19–211
John 4:16	Revelation 19:10	

The Resurrection

Opening Thought

1) Which Bible event would you most like to have been an eyewitness of:
- creation
- the flood
- the exodus
- the birth of Christ
- the crucifixion
- the resurrection
- some other?

Why?

_____

_____

2) What is the most mournful funeral you've ever witnessed? What made it so sad? What was the most joyous and hopeful funeral you've ever attended? What made it such a time of encouragement?

_____

_____

3) If you polled your neighbors (up and down your street) regarding their views of the afterlife, what sort of opinions do you think you'd uncover?

_____

_____

Background of the Passage

Just as the heart pumps life-giving blood to every part of the body, so the truth of the resurrection gives life to every other area of gospel truth. The resurrection is the pivot on which all of Christianity turns and without which none of the other truths would much matter. Without the resurrection, Christianity would be so much wishful thinking, taking its place alongside all other human philosophy and religious speculation.

The doctrinal problem on which this chapter focuses was not the Corinthians' disbelief in Christ's resurrection, but confusion about their own. Paul was not trying to convince them that Christ rose from the dead but that one day they, too, would be raised with him to eternal life. Nevertheless, to lay the foundation, in the first eleven verses he reviews the evidences for Jesus' resurrection, a truth he acknowledges they already believed (vv. 1, 11).

Verses 12–34 show the implications of denying the resurrection. Verses 35–49 deal with another troubling issue, the question of how a general resurrection could be possible. In verses 50–58, Paul proclaims the marvelous victory that resurrection will bring for those who are Christ's.

His closing "victory song" has been put to music in such masterpieces as Handel's *Messiah* and Brahms's *Requiem*, and in many ways it is more appropriate to be sung than preached. Praising God in anticipation of resurrection, the apostle proclaims the great transformation, the great triumph, and the great thanksgiving that the raising of God's saints will bring, and then gives a great exhortation for holy living until that day comes.

Bible Passage

Read 1 Corinthians 15:1–58, noting the key words and definitions to the right of the passage.

1 Corinthians 15:1–58

¹ Moreover, brethren, I declare to you the gospel which I preached to you, which also you received and in which you stand,

² by which also you are saved, if you hold fast that word which I preached to you—unless you believed in vain.

preached . . . received . . . stand (vv. 1–2)—This was not a new message. They had heard of the resurrection, believed in it, and had been saved by it.

unless you believed in vain (v. 2)—By this qualifying statement, Paul recognized and called to their attention that some may have had a

3 *For I delivered to you first of all that which I also received: that Christ died for our sins according to the Scriptures,*

4 *and that He was buried, and that He rose again the third day according to the Scriptures,*

5 *and that He was seen by Cephas, then by the twelve.*

6 *After that He was seen by over five hundred brethren at once, of whom the greater part remain to the present, but some have fallen asleep.*

7 *After that He was seen by James, then by all the apostles.*

8 *Then last of all He was seen by me also, as by one born out of due time.*

9 *For I am the least of the apostles, who am not worthy to be called an apostle, because I persecuted the church of God.*

10 *But by the grace of God I am what I am, and His grace toward me was not in vain; but I labored more abundantly than they all, yet not I, but the grace of God which was with me.*

11 *Therefore, whether it was I or they, so we preach and so you believed.*

12 *Now if Christ is preached that He has been raised from the dead, how do some among you say that there is no resurrection of the dead?*

13 *But if there is no resurrection of the dead, then Christ is not risen.*

14 *And if Christ is not risen, then our preaching is empty and your faith is also empty.*

15 *Yes, and we are found false witnesses of God, because we have testified of God that He raised up Christ, whom He did not raise up—if in fact the dead do not rise.*

16 *For if the dead do not rise, then Christ is not risen.*

17 *And if Christ is not risen, your faith is futile; you are still in your sins!*

18 *Then also those who have fallen asleep in Christ have perished.*

shallow, non-saving faith. Some believed only as the demons believed (James 2:19), that is, they were convinced the gospel was true, but had no love for God, Christ, and righteousness. True believers "hold fast" to the gospel.

according to the Scriptures (vv. 3–4)—The Old Testament spoke of the suffering and resurrection of Christ (see Luke 24:25–27; Acts 2:25–31; 26:22–23). Jesus, Peter, and Paul quoted or referred to Old Testament passages regarding the work of Christ, including Psalm 22; Isaiah 53.

seen by (vv. 5–7)—The testimony of eyewitnesses, recorded in the New Testament, was added to support the reality of the resurrection. These included (1) John and Peter together, but probably also separately before; (2) the Twelve; (3) the five hundred, only referred to here; (4) James, either one of the two so-named apostles (son of Zebedee or son of Alphaeus; see Mark 3:17–18), or even James the half-brother of the Lord, the author of the epistle by that name and the key leader in the Jerusalem church (Acts 15:13–21); and (5) the apostles (John 20:19–29). Such unspecified appearances occurred over a forty-day period (Acts 1:3) to all the apostles.

born out of due time (v. 8)— Paul was saved too late to be one of the twelve apostles. Christ had ascended before he was converted. But through a miraculous appearance (Acts 18:9–10; 23:11; 2 Cor. 12:1–7), Christ revealed Himself to Paul and, according to divine purpose, Paul was made an apostle. See note on 1:1. He was "last of all" the apostles and felt himself to be the "least" (vv. 9–10; 1 Tim. 1:12–17).

labored more . . . they all (v. 10)—In terms of years and extent of ministry, he exceeded all those named (vv. 5–7). John outlived him but did not have the extensive ministry of Paul.

19 *If in this life only we have hope in Christ, we are of all men the most pitiable.*

20 *But now Christ is risen from the dead, and has become the firstfruits of those who have fallen asleep.*

21 *For since by man came death, by Man also came the resurrection of the dead.*

22 *For as in Adam all die, even so in Christ all shall be made alive.*

23 *But each one in his own order: Christ the first-fruits, afterward those who are Christ's at His coming.*

24 *Then comes the end, when He delivers the king-dom to God the Father, when He puts an end to all rule and all authority and power.*

25 *For He must reign till He has put all enemies under His feet.*

26 *The last enemy that will be destroyed is death.*

27 *For "He has put all things under His feet." But when He says "all things are put under Him," it is evident that He who put all things under Him is excepted.*

28 *Now when all things are made subject to Him, then the Son Himself will also be subject to Him who put all things under Him, that God may be all in all.*

29 *Otherwise, what will they do who are baptized for the dead, if the dead do not rise at all? Why then are they baptized for the dead?*

30 *And why do we stand in jeopardy every hour?*

31 *I affirm, by the boasting in you which I have in Christ Jesus our Lord, I die daily.*

32 *If, in the manner of men, I have fought with beasts at Ephesus, what advantage is it to me? If the dead do not rise, "Let us eat and drink, for tomorrow we die!"*

33 *Do not be deceived: "Evil company corrupts good habits."*

34 *Awake to righteousness, and do not sin; for some do not have the knowledge of God. I speak this to your shame.*

some among you say (v. 12)—The Corinthian Christians believed in Christ's resurrection, or else they could not have been Christians (see John 6:44; 11:25; Acts 4:12; 2 Cor. 4:14; 1 Thess. 4:16). But some had particular difficulty accepting and understanding the resurrection of believers. Some of this confusion was a result of their experiences with pagan philosophies and reli-gions. A basic tenet of much of ancient Greek philosophy was dual-ism, which taught that everything physical was intrinsically evil; so the idea of a resurrected body was repulsive and disgusting (Acts 17:32). In addition, perhaps some Jews in the Corinthian church for-merly may have been influenced by the Sadducees, who did not believe in the resurrection even though it is taught in the Old Testament (Job 19:26; Ps. 16:8–11; 17:15; Dan. 12:2). On the other hand, Christ's own teaching on the resurrection was extensive (John 5:28, 29; 6:44; 11:25; 14:19), and it was the theme of the apostolic preaching (Acts 4:1–2). In spite of that clarity, the church at Corinth was in doubt about the resurrection.

still in your sins (v. 17)—See Acts 5:30–31.

fallen asleep (v. 18)—A common euphemism for death (see vv. 6, 20; 11:30; Matt. 27:52; Acts 7:60). This is not soul sleep, in which the body dies and the soul, or spirit, suppos-edly rests in unconsciousness.

most pitiable (v. 19)—This is because of the sacrifices made in this life in light of the hope of life to come. If there is no life to come, we would be better "to eat, drink and be merry" before we die.

firstfruits (v. 20)—This speaks of the first installment of harvest to eternal life, in which Christ's resur-rection will precipitate and guaran-tee that all of the saints who have died will also be resurrected.

man . . . Man (vv. 21–22)—

35 But someone will say, "How are the dead raised up? And with what body do they come?"

36 Foolish one, what you sow is not made alive unless it dies.

37 And what you sow, you do not sow that body that shall be, but mere grain—perhaps wheat or some other grain.

38 But God gives it a body as He pleases, and to each seed its own body.

39 All flesh is not the same flesh, but there is one kind of flesh of men, another flesh of animals, another of fish, and another of birds.

40 There are also celestial bodies and terrestrial bodies; but the glory of the celestial is one, and the glory of the terrestrial is another.

41 There is one glory of the sun, another glory of the moon, and another glory of the stars; for one star differs from another star in glory.

42 So also is the resurrection of the dead. The body is sown in corruption, it is raised in incorruption.

43 It is sown in dishonor, it is raised in glory. It is sown in weakness, it is raised in power.

44 It is sown a natural body, it is raised a spiritual body. There is a natural body, and there is a spiritual body.

45 And so it is written, "The first man Adam became a living being." The last Adam became a life-giving spirit.

46 However, the spiritual is not first, but the natural, and afterward the spiritual.

47 The first man was of the earth, made of dust; the second Man is the Lord from heaven.

48 As was the man of dust, so also are those who are made of dust; and as is the heavenly Man, so also are those who are heavenly.

49 And as we have borne the image of the man of dust, we shall also bear the image of the heavenly Man.

50 Now this I say, brethren, that flesh and blood cannot inherit the kingdom of God; nor does corruption inherit incorruption.

Adam, who through his sin brought death on the whole human race, was human. So was Christ, who by His resurrection brought life to the race.

all . . . all (v. 22)—The two "alls" are alike only in the sense that they both apply to descendants. The second "all" applies only to believers (see Gal. 3:26, 29; Eph. 3:6; see Acts 20:32; Titus 3:7) and does not imply universalism (the salvation of everyone without faith). Countless other passages clearly teach the eternal punishment of the unbelieving (e.g., Matt. 5:29; 10:28; Luke 16:23; 2 Thess. 1:9; Rev. 20:15).

in his own order (v. 23)—Christ was first, as the firstfruits of the resurrection harvest (vv. 20–23a). Because of His resurrection, "those who are Christ's" will be raised and enter the eternal heavenly state in three stages at Christ's coming (see Matt. 24:36, 42, 44, 50; 25:13): (1) those who have come to saving faith from Pentecost to the Rapture will be joined by living saints at the rapture to meet the Lord in the air and ascend to heaven (1 Thess. 4:16–17); (2) those who come to faith during the Tribulation, with the Old Testament saints as well, will be raised up to reign with Him during the Millennium (Rev. 20:4; see Dan. 12:2; Is. 26:19, 20); and (3) those who die during the millennial kingdom may well be instantly transformed at death into their eternal bodies and spirits. The only people left to be raised will be the ungodly, and that will occur at the end of the Millennium at the Great White Throne Judgment of God (see Rev. 20:11–15; see John 5:28–29), which will be followed by eternal hell (Rev. 21:8).

Then comes the end (v. 24)— This third aspect of the resurrection involves the restoration of the earth to the rule of Christ, the rightful King. "End" can refer not only to what is over, but to what is complete and fulfilled.

He delivers the kingdom to

51 Behold, I tell you a mystery: We shall not all sleep, but we shall all be changed—

52 in a moment, in the twinkling of an eye, at the last trumpet. For the trumpet will sound, and the dead will be raised incorruptible, and we shall be changed.

53 For this corruptible must put on incorruption, and this mortal must put on immortality.

54 So when this corruptible has put on incorruption, and this mortal has put on immortality, then shall be brought to pass the saying that is written: "Death is swallowed up in victory."

55 "O Death, where is your sting?
O Hades, where is your victory?"

56 The sting of death is sin, and the strength of sin is the law.

57 But thanks be to God, who gives us the victory through our Lord Jesus Christ.

58 Therefore, my beloved brethren, be steadfast, immovable, always abounding in the work of the Lord, knowing that your labor is not in vain in the Lord.

God (v. 24)—In the culmination of the world's history, after Christ has taken over the restored world for His Father and reigned for a thousand years, all things will be returned to the way they were designed by God to be in the sinless glory of the new heavens and new earth (see Rev. 21–22).

end to all rule (v. 24)—Christ will permanently conquer every enemy of God and take back the earth that He created and that is rightfully His. During the Millennium, under Christ's rule, rebelliousness will still exist and Christ will have to "rule them with a rod of iron" (Rev. 19:15). At the end of that a thousand years, Satan will be unleashed briefly to lead a final insurrection against God (Rev. 20:7–9). But with all who follow his hatred of God and Christ, he will be banished to hell with his fallen angels to suffer forever in the lake of fire (Rev. 20:10–15).

all enemies under His feet (v. 25)—This figure comes from the common practice of kings always sitting enthroned above their subjects, so that when the subjects bowed or kneeled, they were lower than the sovereign's feet. With enemies, the monarch might put his foot on the neck of a conquered ruler, symbolizing that enemy's total subjugation. In the millennial kingdom, Christ's foes will be in subjection to Him.

last enemy . . . death (vv. 26–27)—Christ has broken the power of Satan, who held the power of death (Heb. 2:14), at the cross. But Satan will not be permanently divested of his weapon of death until the end of the Millennium. At that point, having fulfilled completely the prophecy of Ps. 8:6 (v. 27a), Christ then will deliver the kingdom to His Father, and the eternal glory of Rev. 21–22 will begin.

it is evident (v. 27)—Lest anyone misunderstand what should be "evident," Paul does not mean by "all things being put under Christ," that God the Father is so included. It is actually the Father who gave Christ His authority (Matt. 28:18; John 5:26–27) and whom the Son perfectly serves.

all in all (v. 28)—Christ will continue to rule because His reign is eternal (Rev. 11:15), but He will reign in His former, full, and glorious place within the Trinity, subject to God (v. 28) in the way eternally designed for Him in full Trinitarian glory.

baptized for the dead (v. 29)—This difficult verse has numerous possible interpretations. Other Scripture passages, however, clarify certain things that it does not mean. It does not teach, for example, that a dead person can be saved by another person's being baptized on his behalf, because baptism never has a part in a person's salvation (Eph. 2:8; see Rom. 3:28; 4:3; 6:3–4). A reasonable view seems to be that "they . . . who are baptized" refers to living believers who give outward testimony to their faith in baptism by water because they were first drawn to Christ by the exemplary lives, faithful influence, and witness of believers who had subsequently died. Paul's point is that if there is no resurrection and no life after death, then why are people coming to Christ to follow the hope of those who have died?

I die daily (vv. 30–31)—Paul continually risked his life in self-sacrificing ministry. Why would he risk death daily, even hourly, if there were no life after death, no reward, and no eternal joy for all his pain?

beasts at Ephesus (v. 32)—This refers perhaps to literal wild animals, or, metaphorically, to the fierce crowd of Ephesians incited against him by Demetrius (Acts 19:23–34). In either case, these were life-threatening dangers (see 2 Cor. 11:23–28).

eat . . . drink . . . die (v. 32)—This direct quote from Is. 22:13 reflects the hopelessness of the backslidden Israelites. Cf. Heb. 11:33–34, 38 for a litany of sufferers who were willing to die because they looked forward to resurrection (v. 35).

Evil company (vv. 33–34)—The Greek term behind this word can also refer to a spoken message. By word or example, evil friends are a corrupting influence. Hope in the resurrection is sanctifying; it leads to godly living, not corruption. Some in the church did not know God and were a corrupting influence, but not for those who hoped for life in God's presence.

what you sow . . . dies (vv. 36–38)—When a seed is planted in the ground it dies; decomposing, it ceases to exist in its seed form, but life comes from inside that dead seed (see John 12:24). Just as God gives a new body to that plant that rises from the dead seed, so He can give a resurrection body to a man who dies.

mystery (v. 51)—This term refers to truth hidden in the past and revealed in the New Testament. See notes on 2:7. In this case, the rapture of the church was never revealed in the Old Testament. It was first mentioned in John 14:1–3, when it is specifically explained, and is detailed in 1 Thessalonians 4:13–18.

sleep (v. 51)—See note on v. 18.

twinkling of an eye (v. 52)—This was Paul's way of showing how brief the "moment" will be. The Greek word for "twinkling" refers to any rapid movement. Since the eye can move more rapidly than any other part of our visible bodies, it seems to well illustrate the sudden transformation of raptured believers.

trumpet will sound (v. 52)—to herald the end of the church era, when all believers will be removed from the earth at the rapture (1 Thess. 4:16)

dead . . . raised (v. 52)—According to 1 Thess. 4:16, they are first, and the living saints follow (1 Thess. 4:17).

death, where is your sting (v. 55)—Paul enhanced his joy at the reality of resurrection by quoting from Is. 25:8 and Hos. 13:14. The latter quote taunts death as if it were a bee whose sting was removed. That sting was the sin that was exposed by the law of God but conquered by Christ in His death.

Understanding the Text

4) What eyewitness evidence did Paul cite as proof of Christ's resurrection?

_____

_____

(verses to consider: Matt. 28:9; Mark 16:9; Luke 24:31–39; John 20:19–20; Acts 1:22)

5) How does the Old Testament support the New Testament doctrine of the resurrection?

_____

_____

(verses to consider: Ps. 16:8–11; Ps. 22; Is. 53; Hos. 6:2)

6) According to Paul, if Christ had never risen from the dead, what would be the consequences (vv. 13–19)?

_____

_____

7) How does the truth of the resurrection provide an incentive for both service and sanctification (vv. 30–34)?

_____

_____

(verses to consider: Rom. 8:18; Heb. 11:32–40)

Cross Reference

Read 1 Thessalonians 4:13–18.

13 But I do not want you to be ignorant, brethren, concerning those who have fallen asleep, lest you sorrow as others who have no hope.

¹⁴ *For if we believe that Jesus died and rose again, even so God will bring with Him those who sleep in Jesus.*

¹⁵ *For this we say to you by the word of the Lord, that we who are alive and remain until the coming of the Lord will by no means precede those who are asleep.*

¹⁶ *For the Lord Himself will descend from heaven with a shout, with the voice of an archangel, and with the trumpet of God. And the dead in Christ will rise first.*

¹⁷ *Then we who are alive and remain shall be caught up together with them in the clouds to meet the Lord in the air. And thus we shall always be with the Lord.*

¹⁸ *Therefore comfort one another with these words.*

Exploring the Meaning

8) What does this passage say about the future resurrection of the righteous?

_____

_____

(verses to consider: John 5:28–29; 2 Cor.5:1–5; Rev. 20:6)

9) Read Romans 5:12–17. How did God finally and completely take away the sting of death?

_____

_____

(verses to consider: Hos. 13:14; Heb. 2:14–15; Rev. 20:14; 21:4)

10) Read Philippians 3:20–21. What will our resurrection bodies be like?

_____

_____

(verse to consider: 1 John 3:2)

Summing Up . . .

"The coming resurrection is the hope and motivation of the church and of all believers. Whatever happens to our present bodies—whether they are healthy or unhealthy, beautiful or plain, short-lived or long-lived, or whether they are indulged or tortured-they are not our permanent bodies, and we should not hold them too dearly. Our blessed hope and assurance is that these created natural bodies one day will be recreated as spiritual bodies. Although we have only a glimpse of what those new bodies will be like, it should be enough to know that 'we shall be like Him.' "—*John MacArthur*

Reflecting on the Text

11) How does the certainty of Christ's resurrection give you hope and strength today?

_____

_____

12) How can the truths in this chapter bring comfort and hope to the heart of someone who has lost a believing loved one?

_____

_____

13) How are your priorities and choices altered as a result of having learned/been reminded about Christ's resurrection (as well as your own)?

_____

_____

Recording Your Thoughts

_____

_____

For further study, see the following passages:

Matthew 25:41, 46	John 8:31; 14:19	Acts 9:1–8
Romans 4:24–25	Romans 5:12–19	2 Corinthians 13:5
Galatians 4:7	1 Peter 1:3–4	2 Peter 3:4
1 John 2:24; 3:2–3	2 John 9	

Stewardship in the Church

1 Corinthians 16:1–4

Opening Thought

1) Recent polls suggest that the average churchgoer only gives about 2–3 percent of his/her income to church or charities. Why do you think this is the case? What do you think this fact reveals?

_____

_____

2) Why is our handling of money such a good barometer of our own beliefs and convictions?

_____

_____

3) If every other family/person in your church gave exactly what you give, what would be the financial health of your church?
- bankrupt!
- forced to cut positions and ministries
- able to maintain the status quo, but not able to expand its ministry
- possessing the resources with which to shake the world for Christ!

4) If you were a pastor or leader of a congregation, how would you address the whole "giving situation"? What sort of things would you do to motivate people? What would you not do?

_____

_____

Background of the Passage

With chapter 16 Paul makes a radical change from the doctrinal to the practical. After discussing the resurrection in great detail, he ends the letter with several exhortations in regard to giving, doing the Lord's work, faithful living and love within the Christian fellowship. He brings us rather abruptly from the future life back to the present life.

Yet the life to come is far from unrelated to living here and now. What lies ahead in resurrection glory lays great responsibility on the present. If we truly believe we are going to leave this world and that our bodies one day will be transformed and perfectly united with our spirits to live all eternity with God our concern should be to lay up treasures in heaven while we are on earth (Matt. 6:20).

The first practical issue of Christian living Paul discusses in chapter 16 is that of giving. In verses 1–4 he presents the purpose, the principles, the protection, and the perspective of Christian giving.

Bible Passage

Read 1 Corinthians 16:1–4, noting the key words and definitions to the right of the passage.

1 Corinthians 16:1–4

¹ *Now concerning the collection for the saints, as I have given orders to the churches of Galatia, so you must do also:*

² *On the first day of the week let each one of you lay something aside, storing up as he may prosper, that there be no collections when I come.*

³ *And when I come, whomever you approve by your letters I will send to bear your gift to Jerusalem.*

⁴ *But if it is fitting that I go also, they will go with me.*

collection (v. 1)—An offering for destitute believers in the overpopulated, famine-stricken city of Jerusalem (v. 3). Paul had previously solicited funds from the churches of Galatia, Macedonia, and Achaia.

first day of the week (v. 2)—This evidences that the early church met on Sunday. The point is that giving must occur regularly, not just when one feels generous, particularly led to do so, or instructed to do so for some special purpose.

as he may prosper (v. 2)—No required amount or percentage for giving to the Lord's work is specified in the New Testament. All giving to the Lord is to be free-will giving and completely discretionary (see Luke 6:38; 2 Cor. 9:6–8). This is not to be confused with the Old Testament required giving of three tithes (which totaled about 23 percent annually to fund the national government of Israel, take care of public festivals, and provide welfare). Modern parallels to the Old Testament tithe are found in the taxation system of most countries (Rom. 13:6). New Testament giving to God was not regulated as to amount.

if it is fitting (vv. 3–4)—This matter of getting the money to Jerusalem was important enough for Paul to go, if necessary.

Understanding the Text

5) What did Paul mean when he spoke of the "collection for the saints"?

_____

_____

_____

_____

_____

(verses to consider: Acts 11:28–30; Rom. 15:26)

6) What amount does the New Testament stipulate that believers must give? How does this compare with Old Testament requirements under the law?

_____

_____

_____

_____

_____

(verses to consider: Lev. 27:30; Num. 18:21–26; Deut. 14:28–29; Mal. 3:8–10)

7) What is the biblical emphasis—the amount of one's gift or the spirit in which it is given?

_____

_____

_____

_____

_____

(verses to consider: Ex. 25:1–2; 35:21; Prov. 3:9–10; 11:24)

Cross Reference

Read 2 Cor.8:1–9:15.

1 Moreover, brethren, we make known to you the grace of God bestowed on the churches of Macedonia:

2 that in a great trial of affliction the abundance of their joy and their deep poverty abounded in the riches of their liberality.

3 For I bear witness that according to their ability, yes, and beyond their ability, they were freely willing,

4 imploring us with much urgency that we would receive the gift and the fellowship of the ministering to the saints.

5 And not only as we had hoped, but they first gave themselves to the Lord, and then to us by the will of God.

6 So we urged Titus, that as he had begun, so he would also complete this grace in you as well.

7 But as you abound in everything—in faith, in speech, in knowledge, in all diligence, and in your love for us—see that you abound in this grace also.

8 I speak not by commandment, but I am testing the sincerity of your love by the diligence of others.

9 For you know the grace of our Lord Jesus Christ, that though He was rich, yet for your sakes He became poor, that you through His poverty might become rich.

10 And in this I give advice: It is to your advantage not only to be doing what you began and were desiring to do a year ago;

11 but now you also must complete the doing of it; that as there was a readiness to desire it, so there also may be a completion out of what you have.

12 For if there is first a willing mind, it is accepted according to what one has, and not according to what he does not have.

13 For I do not mean that others should be eased and you burdened;

14 but by an equality, that now at this time your abundance may supply their lack, that their abundance also may supply your lack—that there may be equality.

15 As it is written, "He who gathered much had nothing left over, and he who gathered little had no lack."

¹⁶ But thanks be to God who puts the same earnest care for you into the heart of Titus.

¹⁷ For he not only accepted the exhortation, but being more diligent, he went to you of his own accord.

¹⁸ And we have sent with him the brother whose praise is in the gospel throughout all the churches,

¹⁹ and not only that, but who was also chosen by the churches to travel with us with this gift, which is administered by us to the glory of the Lord Himself and to show your ready mind,

²⁰ avoiding this: that anyone should blame us in this lavish gift which is administered by us—

²¹ providing honorable things, not only in the sight of the Lord, but also in the sight of men.

²² And we have sent with them our brother whom we have often proved diligent in many things, but now much more diligent, because of the great confidence which we have in you.

²³ If anyone inquires about Titus, he is my partner and fellow worker concerning you. Or if our brethren are inquired about, they are messengers of the churches, the glory of Christ.

²⁴ Therefore show to them, and before the churches the proof of your love and of our boasting on your behalf.

^{9:1} Now concerning the ministering to the saints, it is superfluous for me to write to you;

² for I know your willingness, about which I boast of you to the Macedonians, that Achaia was ready a year ago; and your zeal has stirred up the majority.

³ Yet I have sent the brethren, lest our boasting of you should be in vain in this respect, that, as I said, you may be ready;

⁴ lest if some Macedonians come with me and find you unprepared, we (not to mention you!) should be ashamed of this confident boasting.

⁵ Therefore I thought it necessary to exhort the brethren to go to you ahead of time, and prepare your generous gift beforehand, which you had previously promised, that it may be ready as a matter of generosity and not as a grudging obligation.

⁶ But this I say: He who sows sparingly will also reap sparingly, and he who sows bountifully will also reap bountifully.

⁷ So let each one give as he purposes in his heart, not grudgingly or of necessity; for God loves a cheerful giver.

⁸ And God is able to make all grace abound toward you, that you, always having all sufficiency in all things, may have an abundance for every good work.

⁹ As it is written:

"He has dispersed abroad,
He has given to the poor;
His righteousness endures forever."

¹⁰ Now may He who supplies seed to the sower, and bread for food, supply and
multiply the seed you have sown and increase the fruits of your righteousness,

¹¹ while you are enriched in everything for all liberality, which causes thanksgiving
through us to God.

¹² For the administration of this service not only supplies the needs of the saints,
but also is abounding through many thanksgivings to God,

¹³ while, through the proof of this ministry, they glorify God for the obedience of
your confession to the gospel of Christ, and for your liberal sharing with them
and all men,

¹⁴ and by their prayer for you, who long for you because of the exceeding grace of
God in you.

¹⁵ Thanks be to God for His indescribable gift!

Exploring the Meaning

8) What practical principles for giving are discussed in these two chapters?

_____

_____

_____

_____

_____

9) Read 1 Timothy 6:7–11, 17–19. What do these verses say about our view
and use of money in this present world?

_____

_____

_____

_____

(verses to consider: Ps. 24:1; Mal. 3:10; Luke 6:38; Acts 2:44–45; 4:34–35)

10) Read Luke 21:1–4. What truth did Jesus teach in this passage? What strikes you about this scene?

_____

_____

_____

_____

_____

Summing Up . . .

"The first day of the week is the day of worship, and how believers handle their money is inextricably related to the depth of their worship. Whether we put money in the offering plate every Sunday or not, weekly worship should remind us of our continual stewardship of the possessions the Lord has entrusted to us. If we do not give properly we cannot worship properly."—*John MacArthur*

Reflecting on the Text

11) Someone has observed, "If you have possessions or riches that you cannot freely give away, you don't own them . . . they own you."

What are some practical steps you can take this week to loosen your grip on money (so that it doesn't grip your own heart)?

_____

_____

_____

_____

12) How do you decide how much to give and to whom you will give? In light of this lesson, what changes do you feel led to make in your giving habits?

_____

_____

_____

_____

_____

13) What considerations do you intend to keep in mind in the future with regard to your giving to the work of the Lord?

_____

_____

_____

_____

_____

Recording Your Thoughts

_____

_____

_____

_____

_____

_____

_____

_____

_____

For further study, see the following passages:

Malachi 1:7–14	Luke 6:38	Acts 20:7
Galatians 6:10	Philippians 4:14–16	1 John 3:17

Doing the Lord's Work in the Lord's Way

Opening Thought

1) If you were writing an epistle to a select group of out-of-town loved ones, friends, and co-workers, what names would likely appear in that letter?

_____

_____

_____

_____

2) If you decided to pass on a few short words of general, spiritual exhortation to your kids, what concise counsel would you give?

_____

_____

_____

_____

3) What are the keys to working effectively with others?

_____

_____

_____

_____

Background of the Passage

A building must be constructed according to the architect's plans and the required building codes. Before it can be used, it must pass inspection to see that the codes were followed. The church's work for the Lord is done in the same way. To truly be His work, what we do must be done according to His plan and code, revealed in Scripture, and must continually be subject to the divine supervision and inspection of the Holy Spirit.

First Corinthians 16:5–12 does not explicitly teach or exhort, except for the advice about receiving Timothy (v. 11). It is more in the form of explanation. Yet we can learn a great deal from these eight verses. The things Paul speaks about here have to do with the work of the Lord, in which all Christians should be deeply involved (15:58).

In 1 Corinthians 16:13–14 Paul gives five final imperatives, five last commands, to the Corinthians. They are to be alert, firm, mature, strong, and loving. These commands are, in many ways, the positive side of what in earlier chapters the apostle had told the Corinthians not to be. Each command can serve as a point of departure for reviewing the epistle.

In many ways, verses 15–24 flow out of and illustrate the command of verse 14: "Let all that you do be done in love." Paul's closing words are not simply niceties that Paul threw in at the end of his letter as a matter of custom or courtesy. As much as any part of Scripture they are part of God's Word and are given to us for a divine purpose. Paul is talking about the all-pervasive love that should mark the fellowship of the church in every locale and every age.

Bible Passage

Read 1 Corinthians 16:5–24, noting the key words and definitions to the right of the passage.

1 Corinthians 16:5-24

5 *Now I will come to you when I pass through Macedonia (for I am passing through Macedonia).*

6 *And it may be that I will remain, or even spend the winter with you, that you may send me on my journey, wherever I go.*

Now I will come to you (v. 5) —At the end of a three-year stay in Ephesus, Paul wrote his letter and probably gave it to Timothy to deliver (v. 10). Paul originally planned to follow Timothy a short while after (4:19), visiting Corinth on the way to and from Macedonia. He had to change his plan and visit only after a longer stay in Ephesus (v. 8), then

118

⁷ For I do not wish to see you now on the way; but I hope to stay a while with you, if the Lord permits.

⁸ But I will tarry in Ephesus until Pentecost.

⁹ For a great and effective door has opened to me, and there are many adversaries.

¹⁰ Now if Timothy comes, see that he may be with you without fear; for he does the work of the Lord, as I also do.

¹¹ Therefore let no one despise him. But send him on his journey in peace, that he may come to me; for I am waiting for him with the brethren.

¹² Now concerning our brother Apollos, I strongly urged him to come to you with the brethren, but he was quite unwilling to come at this time; however, he will come when he has a convenient time.

¹³ Watch, stand fast in the faith, be brave, be strong.

¹⁴ Let all that you do be done with love.

¹⁵ I urge you, brethren—you know the household of Stephanas, that it is the firstfruits of Achaia, and that they have devoted themselves to the ministry of the saints—

¹⁶ that you also submit to such, and to everyone who works and labors with us.

¹⁷ I am glad about the coming of Stephanas, Fortunatus, and Achaicus, for what was lacking on your part they supplied.

¹⁸ For they refreshed my spirit and yours. Therefore acknowledge such men.

¹⁹ The churches of Asia greet you. Aquila and Priscilla greet you heartily in the Lord, with the church that is in their house.

²⁰ All the brethren greet you. Greet one another with a holy kiss.

²¹ The salutation with my own hand—Paul's.

²² If anyone does not love the Lord Jesus Christ, let him be accursed. O Lord, come!

²³ The grace of our Lord Jesus Christ be with you.

²⁴ My love be with you all in Christ Jesus. Amen.

on to Corinth after Macedonia, to stay for a while (vv. 6–7).

many adversaries (v. 9)—Perhaps no New Testament church had such fierce opposition as the one in Ephesus (see 2 Cor. 1:8–10, where Paul described his experience in Ephesus). In spite of that opposition, the door for the gospel was open wide (see 2 Cor. 2:12–13 where Paul also had an open door, but no heart to remain and preach) and Paul stayed. At the end of the experience of opposition described in 2 Corinthians 1:8–10, he wrote 1 Corinthians.

Timothy (v. 10)—Paul had sent him with Erastus to Macedonia (Acts 19:22), and then he was to travel to Corinth, perhaps to carry this epistle (4:17).

without fear (v. 10)—i.e., of intimidation or frustration by believers in Corinth

Apollos (v. 12)—Paul felt Apollos should accompany the other brothers, Timothy and Erastus, to Corinth. Apollos refused, staying in Ephesus longer. Paul respected his convictions.

the faith (v. 13)—the Christian faith, that is, sound doctrine

firstfruits (v. 15)—The members of the household of Stephanas were among the first converts in Corinth, which is located in Achaia, the southern province of Greece. Stephanas was one of the Corinthian believers Paul baptized personally (1:16), and he was visiting with Paul in Ephesus at the time this epistle was written. With Fortunatus and Achaicus (v. 17), he probably delivered the earlier letter from Corinth mentioned in 7:1 (see note there).

Aquila and Priscilla (v. 19)—They had become good friends with Paul, since he stayed in their house during his first ministry in Corinth. He may have stayed with them the entire year and a half.

in their house (v. 19)—The early church used homes of believers for worship and many other activities (see e.g., Acts 2:46; 5:42; 10:23, 27–48; 20:7–8; 28:23).

kiss (v. 20)—A pure expression of Christian love with no sexual overtones.

my own hand (v. 21)—Paul dictated the main part of the letter to a scribe, but finished and signed it himself

Understanding the Text

4) What hopes and plans did Paul disclose at the end of the letter of 1 Corinthians?

_____

_____

_____

5) Why did Paul want to get to Ephesus? What did he expect to face there?

_____

_____

_____

6) Who were Priscilla and Aquila?

_____

_____

_____

(verses to consider: Acts 18:1–3, 18–26; Rom. 16:3–5; 2 Tim. 4:19)

7) What principles for powerful living did Paul conclude with?

_____

_____

_____

_____

Cross Reference

Read 2 Corinthians 13:11–14.

¹¹ *Finally, brethren, farewell. Become complete. Be of good comfort, be of one mind, live in peace; and the God of love and peace will be with you.*
¹² *Greet one another with a holy kiss.*
¹³ *All the saints greet you.*
¹⁴ *The grace of the Lord Jesus Christ, and the love of God, and the communion of the Holy Spirit be with you all. Amen.*

Exploring the Meaning

8) How does the end of 2 Corinthians compare with the closing verses of 1 Corinthians? How does it contrast?

_____

_____

9) Read 1 Peter 4:8. Why is love the greatest need of believers in every era?

_____

_____

10) Read Ephesians 5:21. How does a spirit of submission make for a healthy environment in the church?

_____

_____

(verses to consider: Matt. 20:26–28; Heb. 13:7, 17; 1 Pet. 5:5)

Summing Up . . .

"The love in which we live and witness is ours only because God has given it to us (1 John 4:19). Paul loved because Christ's love controlled him (2 Cor. 5:14). Evangelizing love, or any other manifestation of Christian love, cannot

be generated by the flesh, by our humanness. It is the work of the Spirit to produce and direct our love, and, through it, to bear fruit for God."
—*John MacArthur*

Reflecting on the Text

11) If the Apostle Paul were to address a letter to your local church, what about your congregation would he affirm and what would he rebuke? What are the implications of this for you personally?

_____

_____

12) In what concrete ways can you be a more supportive team player to your church leadership this week?

_____

_____

13) What is the primary truth or principle from this study that you want to study and ponder more?

_____

_____

Recording Your Thoughts

_____

_____

_____

For further study, see the following passages:

Proverbs 25:25	Acts 18:24	Acts 19:1–21
Romans 16:16, 22	2 Corinthians 1:8–16	2 Corinthians 13:12
Philippians 1:27	1 Thessalonians 5:12–13	1 Thessalonians 5:26
1 Timothy 6:12	1 Peter 5:14	Jude 3

The MacArthur Bible Collection

John MacArthur, General Editor

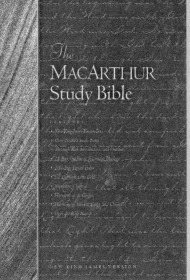

The MacArthur Study Bible

From the moment you pick it up, you'll know it's a classic. Featuring the word-for-word accuracy of the New King James Version, *The MacArthur Study Bible* is perfect for serious study. Pastor/teacher John MacArthur has compiled more than 20,000 study notes, a 200-page topical index and numerous charts, maps, outlines, and articles to create *The MacArthur Study Bible*. This Bible has been crafted with the finest materials in a variety of handsome bindings, including hardcover and indexed bonded leather. Winner of "The 1998 Study Bible of the Year Award."

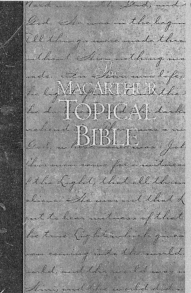

The MacArthur Topical Bible

In the excellent tradition of *Nave's Topical Bible,* this newly created reference book incorporates thousands of topics and ideas, both traditional and contemporary, for believers today and in the new millennium. Carefully researched and prepared by Dr. John MacArthur and the faculty of Masters Seminary, *The MacArthur Topical Bible* will quickly become the reference of choice of all serious Bible students. Using the New King James translation, this Bible is arranged alphabetically by topic and is completely cross-referenced. This exhaustive resource is an indispensible tool for the topical study of God's Word.

The MacArthur Bible Studies

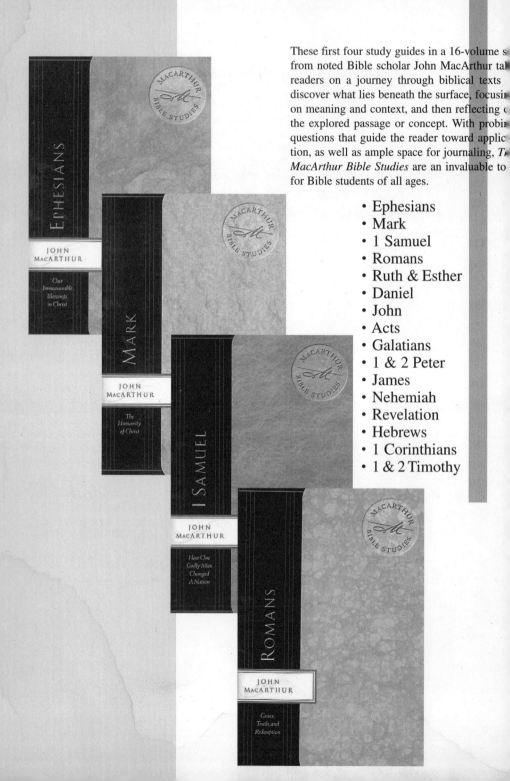

These first four study guides in a 16-volume s
from noted Bible scholar John MacArthur ta
readers on a journey through biblical texts
discover what lies beneath the surface, focusi
on meaning and context, and then reflecting
the explored passage or concept. With probi
questions that guide the reader toward applic
tion, as well as ample space for journaling, *T*
MacArthur Bible Studies are an invaluable to
for Bible students of all ages.

- Ephesians
- Mark
- 1 Samuel
- Romans
- Ruth & Esther
- Daniel
- John
- Acts
- Galatians
- 1 & 2 Peter
- James
- Nehemiah
- Revelation
- Hebrews
- 1 Corinthians
- 1 & 2 Timothy